Michael Price

Excel Functions & Formulas

in easy steps

In easy steps is an imprint of In Easy Steps Limited
16 Hamilton Terrace · Holly Walk · Leamington Spa
Warwickshire · United Kingdom · CV32 4LY
www.ineasysteps.com

Notice of Liability
Every effort has been made to ensure that this book contains accurate
and current information. However, In Easy Steps Limited and the
author shall not be liable for any loss or damage suffered by readers
as a result of any information contained herein.

Trademarks
Microsoft® and Windows® are registered trademarks of Microsoft
Corporation. All other trademarks are acknowledged as belonging to
their respective companies.

In Easy Steps Limited supports The Forest Stewardship Council (FSC),
the leading international forest certification organization. All our titles
that are printed on Greenpeace approved FSC certified paper carry the
FSC logo.

MIX
Paper from
responsible sources
FSC® C020837

Printed and bound in the United Kingdom

ISBN 978-1-84078-881-5

Contents

4   Math & Trig and Logical   57

5   Date & Time and Text   71

6   Financial and Statistical   87

1 Values and Formulas

The power that drives the Excel spreadsheet derives from the formulas and functions in the individual cells. We begin our review of these by examining the values and formulas that may be stored in the cells, and see how Excel can assist in handling these.

Cell Contents

However simple or complex the spreadsheet, its cells will contain one of three possibilities:

- l — Label — Some form of text
- v — Value — Number, with formatting
- b — Blank — Empty cell

Review the cells in this example spreadsheet:

Don't forget

To check the type of cell content, you use the **CELL** function – e.g. to get the type of cell **C3**:
=CELL("type",C3)

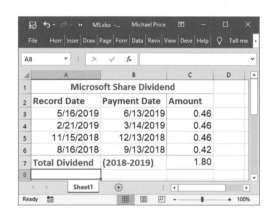

The cells are displayed with their associated formatting applied. For example, the numbers in cells A3:B6 are displayed as dates.

To see the actual contents of the cells:

1 Press **Ctrl** + ` (the grave accent key) or select the **Formulas** tab and click **Show Formulas**

The actual contents of the cells, as entered, are displayed:

Don't forget

This shows the cell contents as entered. For a date, the entered value is converted to the number of days since January 1st, 1900.

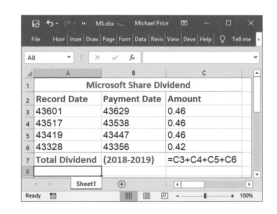

Numbers in the cells are displayed according to the cell format
that has been assigned. The same value can appear in many
different ways – for example:

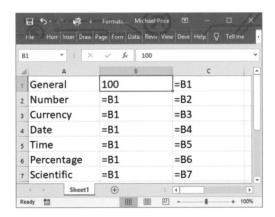

The number 100 takes on significantly different appearances,
depending on the format applied. However, when the cell contents
are referenced, the same underlying value is assigned, irrespective
of the format.

 Press **Ctrl + `**, or select the **Formulas** tab and click **Show
Formulas** to show the actual contents

Cells C1 to C7 are assigned the contents of cells B1 to B7
respectively, and in each case the value of 100 is applied, whatever
the display format may be.

Whenever a cell is referenced, it is the intrinsic value of the cell
that will be made use of.

Values

You can use the **TYPE** function to check the contents of cells. This can identify five possibilities:

- 1 **Number**
- 2 **Text**
- 4 **Logical (True or False)**
- 16 **Error notification**
- 64 **Array**

For example:

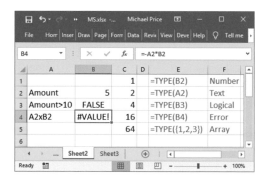

Hot tip

The array identified in cell C5 is actually incorporated as a literal value in the TYPE statement.

Cells such as B4 in the above spreadsheet, or C7 in the first example on page 9, are **formulas**, identified by the initial = (equals sign).

Neither the **CELL** function nor the **TYPE** function will identify a formula as such, but will merely reflect the actual value that the formula produces.

Here are some example formulas:

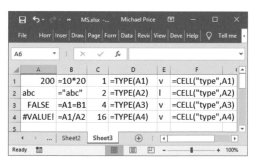

Hot tip

These formulas contain references to a cell/cells (or they could contain literal values), and the values are processed by the operators that are included in the formula.

Here **CELL** identifies value and label contents, while **TYPE** identifies number, text, logical and error contents. If the results of a formula change, the type identified will change to match.

Formulas

Formulas in Excel can be very simple or very complex, but they all have the same basic features:

- **An initial e sign**
  (Tells Excel that a formula follows.)
- **One or more operands**
  (Values or cell references.)
- **One or more operators**
  (Symbols indicating how operands are treated.)

The Annual Budget spreadsheet includes some typical formulas:

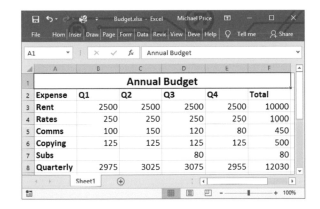

1 Display the cell contents to see the actual formulas

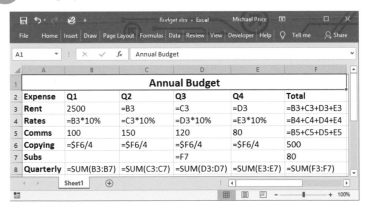

Cells C3 to E3 replicate the adjacent cell. Cells B4 to E4 are percentages of cells B3 to E3. Cells F3 to F5 contain the combined values of the adjacent four cells. Cells B8 to E8 contain the combined values of the five cells above, calculated using the **SUM** function rather than just adding the specific cells.

Operators

Operators used in Excel formulas fall into four groups:

- **Arithmetic**
- **Comparison**
- **Text**
- **Reference**

The actions that operators perform can be applied to literal values, referenced cells or to the values produced by functions.

The operators available, their descriptions and examples of usage:

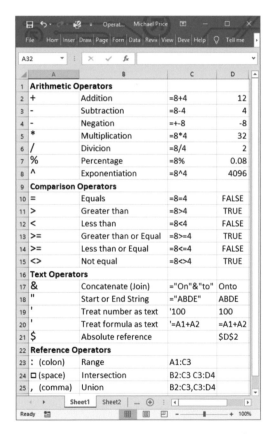

Arithmetic Operators			
+	Addition	=8+4	12
-	Subtraction	=8-4	4
-	Negation	=+-8	-8
*	Multiplication	=8*4	32
/	Divicion	=8/4	2
%	Percentage	=8%	0.08
^	Exponentiation	=8^4	4096
Comparison Operators			
=	Equals	=8=4	FALSE
>	Greater than	=8>4	TRUE
<	Less than	=8<4	FALSE
>=	Greater than or Equal	=8>=4	TRUE
>=	Less than or Equal	=8<=4	FALSE
<>	Not equal	=8<>4	TRUE
Text Operators			
&	Concatenate (Join)	="On"&"to"	Onto
"	Start or End String	="ABDE"	ABDE
'	Treat number as text	'100	100
'	Treat formula as text	'=A1+A2	=A1+A2
$	Absolute reference		D2
Reference Operators			
: (colon)	Range	A1:C3	
☐ (space)	Intersection	B2:C3 C3:D4	
, (comma)	Union	B2:C3,C3:D4	

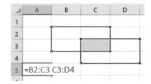

Here is the **Intersection** of two ranges:

=B2:C3 C3:D4

This shows the **Union** of two ranges:

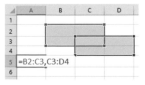

=B2:C3,C3:D4

Each of the **Comparison** operators gives a **Logical** result, which can be either TRUE or FALSE.

The **Reference** operators allow you to select cells from one or two ranges. These cells can then be processed by other operators or functions – for example, to calculate the totals of all the selected cells. **Intersection** selects the cells that are common to two ranges – for example, the overlap. **Union** selects all the cells from both ranges.

Order of Calculation

If there are several operands and operators in a formula, the sequence in which the calculations are performed can be crucial. For example, the formula 4+8^2 could be evaluated from left to right, as 12^2, giving 144. Alternatively, the exponential could be computed first, as 4+64, giving 68.

To avoid any ambiguity, Excel uses a predefined sequence. This operator precedence is as follows:

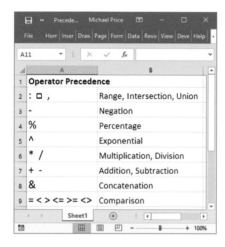

Hot tip

This sequence is known as **PEDMAS** (parentheses, exponential, division, multiplication, addition, subtraction). In Europe it is known as **BODMAS** (brackets, order, division, multiplication, addition, subtraction).

Operators such as * and / that are at the same level could be evaluated in any order. However, Excel chooses to evaluate them from left to right.

You can use parentheses to control the computation. Expressions within the innermost set of parentheses will be calculated first, then Excel works outwards.

Hot tip

You can add parentheses and spaces to formulas, even if they are not strictly necessary, to make them easier to understand.

To illustrate the effects of parentheses, the same formula is shown with various combinations of parentheses:

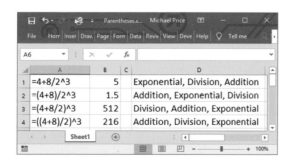

	A	B	C	D
1	=4+8/2^3	5		Exponential, Division, Addition
2	=(4+8)/2^3	1.5		Addition, Exponential, Division
3	=(4+8/2)^3	512		Division, Addition, Exponential
4	=((4+8)/2)^3	216		Addition, Division, Exponential

Beware

The **Negation** operation is treated differently in Excel. Arithmetically the formula -4^2 is -16. However, in Excel, **Negation** is applied before **Exponential** so the formula becomes (-4)^2, which is 16.

Creating Formulas

You can use a combination of typing and selecting to create formulas using the various operators.

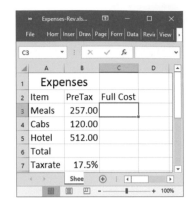

To add a formula to the example Expenses spreadsheet, to calculate the full cost of an item:

1 Double-click cell C3 to select that cell for editing

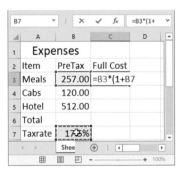

2 Type = and then click the cell B3 (or simply type B3)

3 Type *(1+ and then select or type B7 (the Taxrate)

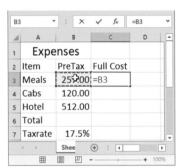

Since Taxrate is a singular value, you'll want to make this an absolute reference, so that you can easily move or copy formulas that use this value.

+B7
+B7
+B$7
+$B7

4 Highlight the cell reference C7 and press F4 once to switch to absolute addressing

14

5 Type the closing parenthesis and press **Enter** to complete the formula

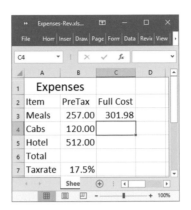

You can also **Copy** the cell with the formula, then select the target cells and use **Paste** to replicate the formula.

You can copy this formula to calculate the full cost of other items, using the fill handle.

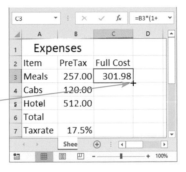

1 Select C3, the cell with the formula, and click the fill handle on the lower right-hand corner

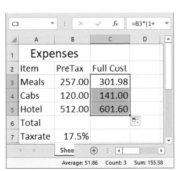

2 Drag down to replicate the formula in the next two cells, C4 and C5, then release the mouse

Since the Taxrate is an absolute reference, it will be replicated unchanged, while the other cell reference will be incremented.

3 Select cell C6 and enter the formula =C3+C4+C5 typing or selecting the required cells, as preferred

4 Press **Enter** to complete the formula

Named References

When you have absolute references in your formulas, you can name them to make their purposes clearer.

To create a name for a particular cell:

Hot tip

Names must start with a letter, an underscore or a backslash. The names can contain letters, numbers, periods and underscores, but no spaces. Case is ignored, and names can be up to 256 characters.

Don't forget

The **Name Manager** shows **Defined Names** for cells, ranges of cells, constants (see page 17) and tables.

Don't forget

Using meaningful names to reference data items may make the intent of the formula easier to understand, as in this example showing expenses with sales tax and gratuities added.

1 Select the cell you want to name – B7, for example

2 Click the **Name** box, on the left of the Formula bar, then type the name – for example, **Taxrate**, then press **Enter**

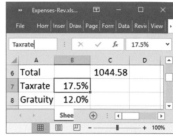

3 Click the **Formulas** tab and select **Name Manager** in the **Defined Names** group to view all the names in the workbook

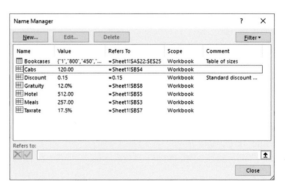

Names create absolute references to cells or ranges of cells. They can be used in formulas and, when these formulas are copied, the references will not be changed.

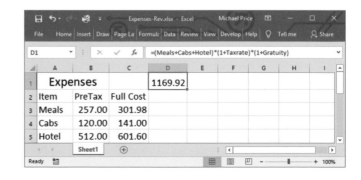

Named Constants

You can name a constant value directly, without having to allocate it to a specific cell. For example, if your formulas require a constant **Discount** rate, you can assign a name and a value as follows:

1 Select **Define Name** from the **Defined Names** group on the **Formulas** tab

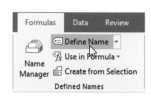

2 The **New Name** dialog box is displayed

3 Select the **Name** box and type the constant name – e.g. **Discount**

4 Set the **Scope** – Workbook or Sheet – and add a description in the **Comment** box, if desired

5 Select the **Refers to** box and replace the cell reference with the required value (e.g. =0.15) and click **OK**

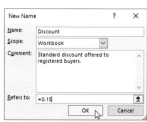

The constants you name can be text as well as numbers. For example, you could define a constant for your company name or address.

You could type a frequently required calculation as a formula in the **Refers to** box, and then use the defined name in other formulas, without having to assign a cell to hold that calculation.

You can now use the defined name in your formulas. Note that the full name and description will be displayed as you start typing the defined constant name. Double-click to enter the name.

Formula Assistance

Excel provides assistance as you enter formulas, to make them easier to construct and to help you check that you have chosen the required values and operations.

Hot tip

Here we calculate a numeric progression and the total and average of its terms. F, D and N are defined names.

1 When you type a defined name, Excel outlines the associated cell or range of cells

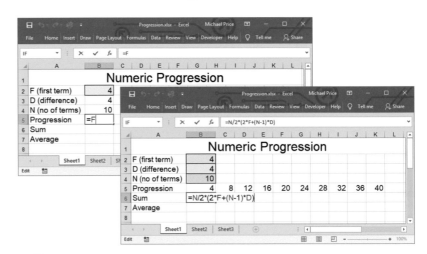

2 With nested calculations, Excel colors matching pairs of parentheses to clarify the operations

Don't forget

Coloring matching pairs of parentheses makes it easier to check the calculation and spot errors such as superfluous parentheses.

`=(N/2*(2*F+(N-1)*D))/N`

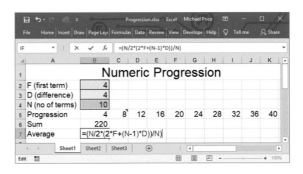

3 If you do make a mistake, such as entering an extra parenthesis as shown above, Excel will detect the error and may offer a correction

Adding Comments

Add notes to a cell – for example, to explain how a particular formula operates. To add such a comment:

1 Select the cell where the comment is meant to display

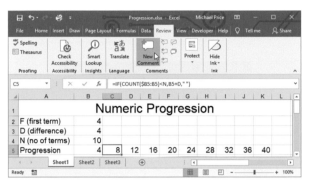

2 Click the **Review** tab and select **New Comment** from the **Comments** group

3 Your username is shown. Delete this if desired, then add your comments, and format the text if you wish

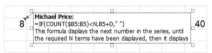

4 Select any other cell to save and close the comment

5 The red flash indicates the presence of a comment, which is displayed when you move the mouse over that cell

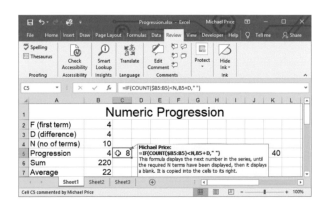

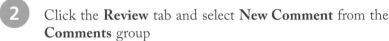
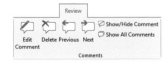

Error Values

If Excel detects a problem for which it is unable to offer a correction, it will place an error value in the cell. Here are some of the error values you may encounter:

1 When a number is too long to fit into a cell, the **Overflow** error is shown. Resolve by widening the cell or choosing a smaller number format

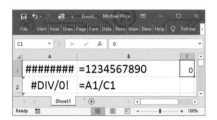

Hot tip

When the error value shows a green flash, select the cell and click the Information icon for more details and options for handling the error.

2 When the formula contains division by a value of zero or by an empty cell, you get a **Divide by Zero** error

3 A **NAME** error implies reference to a deleted name, or to a name that has not been defined

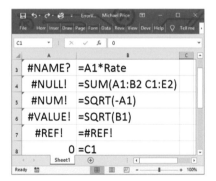

4 A **NULL** error results from referencing the intersection or two ranges that do not overlap

5 You'll get a **NUM** error with invalid arguments, such as a negative number with the square root function, or a **VALUE** error with an argument of the wrong data type

Beware

If the formula has a reference to C1 and you copy the formula upwards, the relative reference changes to C0, which is an invalid cell reference.

6 An invalid reference gives a **REF** error, such as when you copy a formula and get an invalid cell reference

2 Managing Formulas

The main feature for managing your formulas is the Formulas tab on the Excel Ribbon. This offers four groups of commands that help you work with your formulas, understand their actions and correct any errors. You can also access the File tab to change options related to formulas.

The Formulas Tab

You can use groups of commands on the Excel Ribbon to manage your formulas. To display these groups:

1 Select **Formulas** on the **Tab bar**

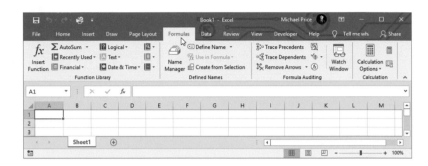

If the **Excel Ribbon** isn't displayed, click the **Ribbon Display Options** button and select **Show Tabs and Commands**.

You will find that the **Formulas** tab normally displays four groups of commands:

- Functions Library
- Defined Names
- Formula Auditing
- Calculation

If you have installed the **Euro Currency Tools** add-in you will find that the **Formulas** tab displays an additional group:

- Solutions

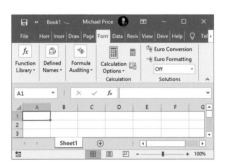

The **Euro Currency Tools** add-in provides conversion and formatting features for the Euro currency. See page 55 for information about installing add-ins.

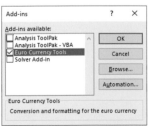

Note that the other add-ins that you may install will not add any groups to the **Formulas** tab.

Formula Auditing

Facilities for managing formulas are in the **Formula Auditing** group. To discover all of the commands this has to offer:

1 Select the **Formulas** tab and review the **Formula Auditing** group

This group provides various individual commands and subsets of commands (indicated by a Down arrow).

2 Click the Down arrow to display the sub commands

 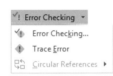

There are 13 commands and sub commands in the group:

- Trace Precedents
- Trace Dependents
- Remove Arrows
    - Remove Arrows
    - Remove Precedent Arrows
    - Remove Dependent Arrows
- Show Formulas
- Error Checking
    - Error Checking...
    - Trace Error
    - Circular References
- Evaluate Formula
- Watch Window

Changes to the worksheet may change inactive commands to active ones. For example, the **Circular References** sub command would be shown as active, not grayed out, should such references get created in the worksheet.

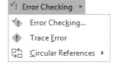

Beware

Depending on the status of the worksheet, some commands or sub commands may not be active and will be grayed out, as with the **Circular References** sub command.

Hot tip

Just to illustrate circular references, we set A1 as =B2 and B2 as =A1. Note that the Circular References sub command lists all the cells involved in the circular reference.

Trace Precedents

You can identify which cells provide data for a particular cell. These cells are known as **precedents**.

To display the precedents for a cell – in this case, the overall total:

1 Select the cell then click the **Formulas** tab, and **Trace Precedents** in the **Formulas Auditing** group

If the selected cell has no formula, an appropriate message will be displayed.

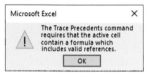

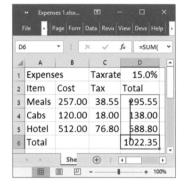

2 Trace arrows indicate the cells that provide data

3 Select **Trace Precedents** again to indicate precedents of precedents, and repeat until there are no further levels

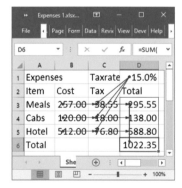

You can click the Down arrow next to **Remove Arrows** and select **Remove Precedent Arrows** explicitly, one level at a time.

In the example worksheet there are three levels of precedents for the selected cell.

4 Click **Formulas** and then click **Remove Arrows** in the **Formulas Auditing** group to cancel the display of trace arrows

Trace Dependents

You can identify which cells use the value in a particular cell. These cells are known as **dependents**.

To display the dependents of a cell – for example, the Taxrate:

1 Select the cell then click the **Formulas** tab, and **Trace Dependents** in the **Formulas Auditing** group

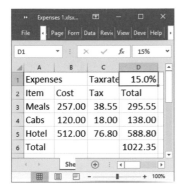 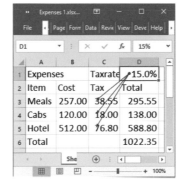

2 Trace arrows indicate the cells that use that data

3 Select **Trace Dependents** again to indicate dependents of dependents, and repeat until there are no further levels

 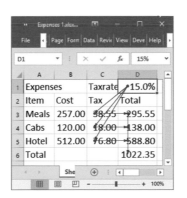

In the example worksheet there are three levels of dependents for the selected cell.

4 Click **Formulas** and then click **Remove Arrows** in the **Formulas Auditing** group to cancel the display of trace arrows for the dependents

Hot tip

If there are no references to the selected cell, a message to that effect will be displayed.

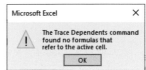

25

Don't forget

You can click the Down arrow next to **Remove Arrows** and select **Remove Dependent Arrows**, one level at a time.

...cont'd

A cell can have both **precedents** and **dependents** – as, for example, the Sales tax – for any of the expenses:

1 Select the cell then select **Trace Precedents** – in this example, just one level is found

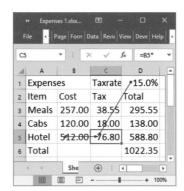 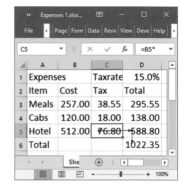

Hot tip

A cell may use a value from another cell, and also provide its value to another part of the worksheet.

2 Alternatively, select **Trace Dependents** – in this case, two levels are shown

3 You can choose to display both sets of trace arrows

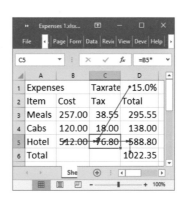 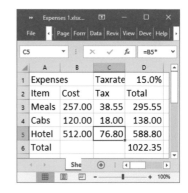

Don't forget

Precedent arrows point toward the cell, while **dependent arrows** point away from the cell, so they are easy to identify.

4 Select **Remove Arrows** to cancel the display of all the trace arrows

5 You can select **Remove Precedent Arrows** or **Remove Dependent Arrows** to remove one level at a time

Show Formulas

Cells normally display the value of the contents, including the computed value of the contained formulas.

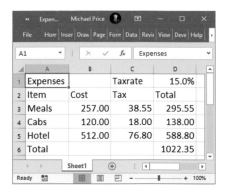

Whatever you enter into a cell, it displays the results after any computation or formatting, rather than the original definition.

However, you can switch to view the cells as originally defined.

1 Select the **Formulas** tab and click **Show Formulas** in the **Formulas Auditing** group

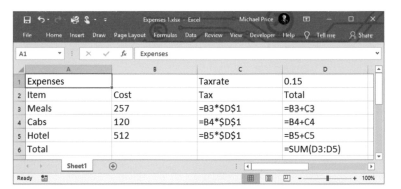

Alternatively, you can press **Ctrl** + ` (the grave accent key) to switch between results and formulas.

2 Repeat the action to switch back to displaying values

3 You can show a specific formula in another cell using the **FORMULATEXT** function

To help make the worksheet easier to understand, you can display a particular formula in another cell – for example, to display the formula defining cell **D6**, you enter the expression **=FORMULATEXT(D6)** in a nearby cell.

Error Checking

Excel provides rules to manage error checking. You can view these rules and, if desired, enable or disable individual rules:

1 Select the **File** tab, click **Options** and select **Formulas**

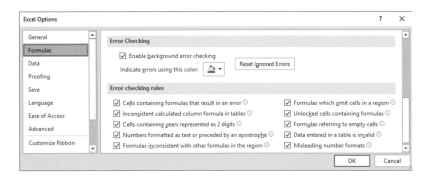

Hot tip

If the worksheet has previously been checked no **Ignored** error will be displayed until you press the **Reset Ignored Errors** button in **Excel Options**.

2 Clear the check boxes for rules you want to disable

3 Select the **Formulas** tab, and click the Down arrow on **Error Checking** in the **Formula Auditing** group

4 Select the entry for **Error Checking...** to review all the errors

Don't forget

You can choose **Ignore Error**, particularly when it is due to incompletely entered data, or correct it via **Edit in Formula Bar**, or skip that error by pressing **Next**.

5 Click **Next** to see each error in turn

6 Click **OK** to finish

Where an error is indicated by a message, you can review it individually:

1 Select a cell with an error message and click **Formulas, Error Checking, Trace Error**

The **Error Checking** commands are very useful when you have a large worksheet where errors and warnings may be off-screen and difficult to spot.

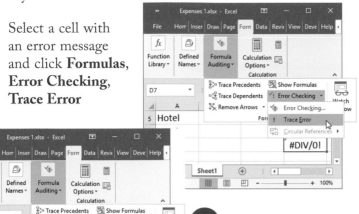

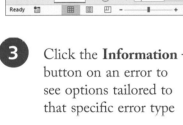

2 Repeat **Trace Error** for the next level

3 Click the **Information** button on an error to see options tailored to that specific error type

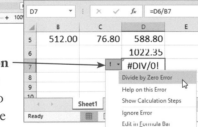

You can get help on this error, review the calculation steps, or edit the formula to correct the error.

4 **Formulas, Error Checking, Circular References** lists the cells that refer to their own contents, directly or indirectly

5 Select a cell and press **F9** to recalculate the worksheet and identify the cells involved in the **Circular References**

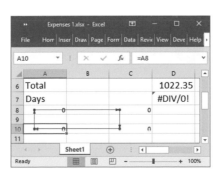

Evaluate Formula

You can use the **Evaluate** command to run a formula one step at a time, to see how it operates. To use this feature:

1 Select the cell with the formula you wish to investigate

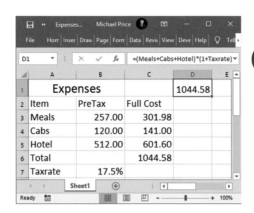

2 Select **Formulas** and click **Evaluate Formula** in the **Formula Auditing** group

3 The formula displays with the first step underlined

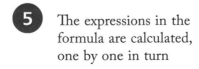

Press the **Step In** button to check the value of a constant, or to see the expansion of range or table names.

Click the **Step Out** button to continue the evaluation.

When you reach the end, click **Restart** to review again, or click **Close** to finish.

4 Press **Evaluate** repeatedly, to run the calculation forwards, a step at a time

5 The expressions in the formula are calculated, one by one in turn

6 You can view the intermediate values as they are displayed

30

Watch Window

If you have values on your worksheet that change over time, you can keep an eye on them, even when you are displaying other parts of the worksheet.

For example, suppose you have a worksheet showing live quotes for share values. To follow the values of specific shares:

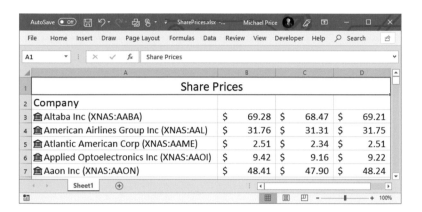

With an Office 365 subscription, Excel can display live share data. You'd enter the stock symbols and select **Data**, **Stocks**, then insert columns such as **High**, **Low** and **Price**.

| AAPL |
| BT |
| F |
| HMC |
| IBM |
| MERC |
| MSFT |
| RYCEY |
| WMT |

To update values, select **Data**, **Refresh All**.

1 Select **Formulas** and click **Watch Window** in the **Formula Auditing** group

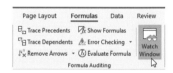

2 The **Watch Window** opens, initially with no watched items

3 Click **Add Watch...**, select a cell to watch, then click **Add**

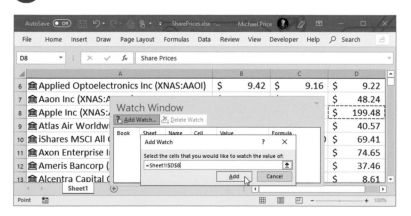

Choose the cells that you want to monitor while working on other sections of the worksheet.

...cont'd

4 The selected cell is placed in the **Watch Window** with its real-time value, plus the cell location information

Hot tip

You can type a cell reference rather than selecting it. You can also select multiple contiguous cells to add them in one operation.

5 Click **Add Watch...**, choose another cell and click **Add**, and repeat this for any other required cell

6 You can monitor the selected cells, wherever you move

Don't forget

You can drag the **Watch Window** to any side of the Excel window, so that it is less likely to obscure the parts of the worksheet you are dealing with.

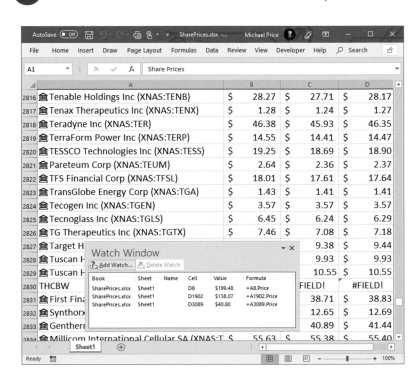

Calculation Options

Whenever you enter or change contents of a cell, Excel normally calculates the formulas in your worksheet that depend on that cell. This is because the default option is **Automatic Calculation**. For very large worksheets with many formulas, this mode of operation may make it very time-consuming to edit or update. In such circumstances, you may wish to change the calculation options.

1 Select the **Formulas** tab and click the **Calculation Options** button in the **Calculation** group

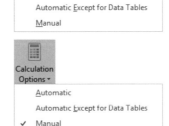

2 Normally you will see **Automatic** selected, for immediate calculation whenever formulas or referenced values change

3 To postpone calculation while you are in the process of editing the worksheet, select the **Manual** option

4 Excel displays **Calculate** in the status bar when you make a change and have uncalculated formulas in the worksheet

5 When you are ready to recalculate, click **Calculate** on the status bar, or select **Calculate Now** or **Calculate Sheet** from the Calculation group

You can use the following shortcut keys to carry out various levels of recalculation:

F9	Calculate formulas in all open workbooks
Shift + F9	Calculate formulas in the active worksheet
Ctrl + Alt + F9	Complete recalculation of all formulas
Ctrl + Alt + Shift + F9	Rebuild calculation dependency tree and perform a complete recalculation

Formulas that are referenced by other formulas are calculated first, followed by those dependent formulas.

When your worksheet features large data tables that may take a long time to recalculate, select the **Automatic, Except for Data Tables** calculation option.

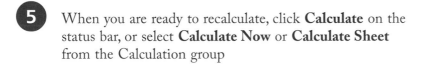

The Calculation mode you select applies to all open workbooks, not just the active workbook.

External References

Sometimes you may find it useful to reference parts of your workbook from another workbook. For example, a **SharePrices** workbook could be used as the source of current prices in a **Portfolio** workbook. Such references are known as **external references** (also known as **links**). To create an external reference:

Hot tip

You can link to individual cells or to ranges of cells in the Source workbook. Whenever the Source workbook changes, the Dependent workbook is changed also.

1 Open the Source and the Dependent workbooks

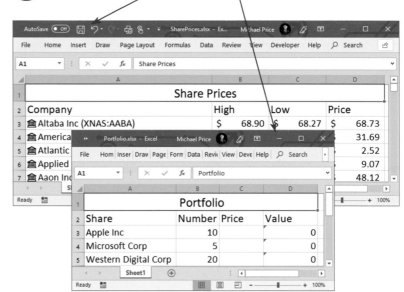

2 Select the cell in the Dependent workbook where you want to place a value from the Source workbook

Hot tip

You can type the reference in the form [File.xlxs]Sheet!Ref where File.xlxs is the Source workbook, Sheet is the worksheet name and Ref is the cell, range or defined name.

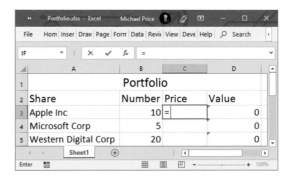

3 Type = to begin the reference then switch across to the Source workbook

4 Click the cell in the Source workbook with the required value, then switch back to the Dependent workbook

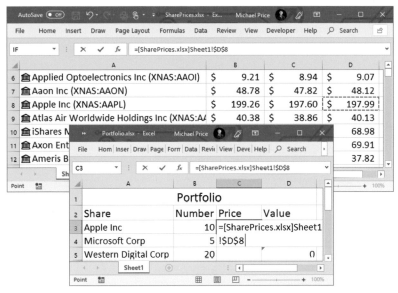

Hot tip

The selected cell is identified as [File.xlxs]Sheet!Ref where Ref is the absolute cell reference.

5 Press **Enter** to link to the Source cell and display its value

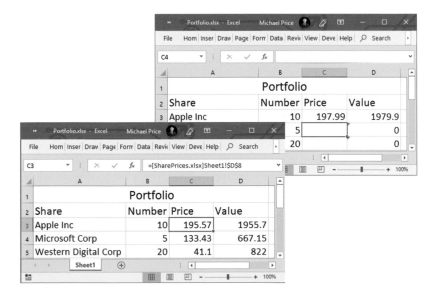

Don't forget

If you close the Source workbook, the reference is amended to display the drive and folder.

6 Repeat the procedure to link to each of the required cells from the Source workbook

Array Formulas

In this example workbook, to display the **Value** for the first item you'd enter the formula **=b3*c3**, and copy it down for other items.

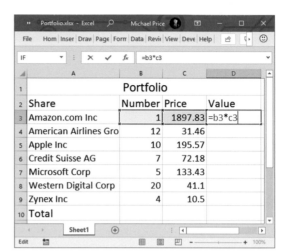

Don't forget

You can replicate the formula to calculate all the values, but this can be time-consuming if there are many entries to complete. Using arrays is a single-step process.

However, Excel offers the **Array** feature to allow you to display all the values in a single operation.

1 Select the Value range **D3:D9** then type the command **=b3:b9*c3:c9**

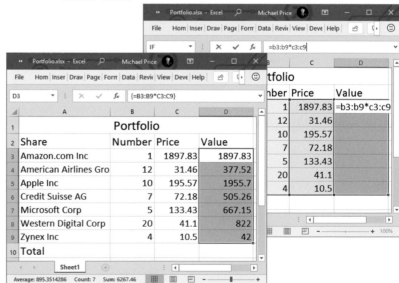

Hot tip

Note that Excel adds curly braces around the formula, which appears in each of the cells as
{=B3:B9*C3:C9}

2 Press **Ctrl + Shift + Enter** and the formula is added to each of the selected cells, which all show the appropriate value

You can use an array formula to calculate the total value of all the items, without having to calculate their individual values and store those values in separate cells in the worksheet.

1 Click the cell that will contain the total and type the formula **=sum(b3:b9*c3:c9)**

Don't forget

When you type the array formula, the ranges that form the arrays are highlighted.

2 Press **Ctrl** + **Shift** + **Enter** and the individual values are calculated and totaled, and the resulting value is shown in the selected cell

Hot tip

Each cell in the one array is multiplied by the matching cell in the other array, and the products are added together to give the overall total.

Note that curly braces are added to the formula, which is stored in the cell as **{=SUM(B2:B9*C3:C9)}**

Dynamic Arrays

Excel has new features that make it easier to work with arrays, and in particular avoid the need to use **Ctrl + Shift + Enter** to complete formulas. For example:

1 Click the cell next to the first pair of values and type the formula **=b3:b9*c3:c9**

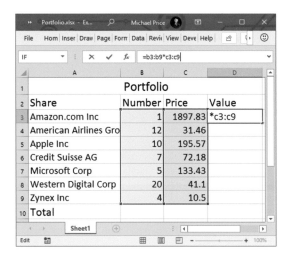

2 Press **Enter**, and all the products are calculated, and the results **spill** into the neighboring blank cell

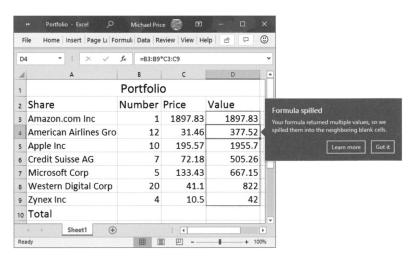

Excel contains a number of new functions that take advantage of dynamic arrays and the Spill feature, including SORT, SORTBY, FILTER, UNIQUE, SEQUENCE and RANDARRAY (see page 62).

Hot tip

When dynamic arrays are supported, there's no need to select all the cells to store the results – they'll automatically spill into adjacent cells.

Hot tip

If the adjacent cells are not all blank, you'll get a **SPILL** error message. Clear the cells, and the spill will complete.

38

Don't forget

Each of the cells in the results contains the array formula
=B3:B9*C3:C9

Note that there are no curly braces added when the dynamic arrays feature is in effect.

3 Functions

Formulas can use Excel Functions as well as operators. Excel Functions are prerecorded formulas that carry out often-used or complex operations. They can be typed, inserted or selected by category from the Function Library. Excel also helps you install add-ins or code your own functions.

Excel Functions

Using the operators in formulas, you can carry out both simple and complex calculations. However, the basic formula facilities make some tasks rather cumbersome. For example, to add the contents of a large number of cells would involve selecting or typing all the cell references, each separated by the Add operator.

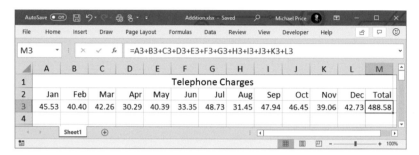

There are a number of categories of functions available with Excel, each with many individual functions. See page 49 for the list of categories supported.

Other tasks may just not be feasible using the operations and techniques that are provided for formulas.

To handle such situations, Excel provides a large number of worksheet functions. These are formulas that Excel has predefined. They extend beyond the arithmetic and text operations you can perform in formulas that you build yourself.

For example, to add the values of a range of cells, Excel provides the **SUM** function to add the values of a range of cells, with just the first and last cells specified.

You can add the contents of a set of cells by selecting the empty cell adjacent to them, and clicking **AutoSum** (see pages 50-51). The range is automatically selected.

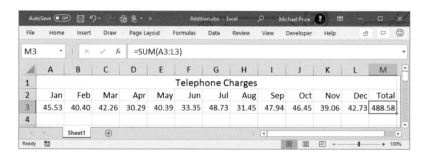

There are functions that involve complex mathematical expressions that would be difficult or impossible to construct using the basic arithmetic operators. For example, Excel's **PMT** function (see page 89) allows you to calculate mortgage repayments.

You can add other functions, not part of Excel as shipped. You can even build your own functions, using **Excel VBA** (Visual Basic).

Check out Excel VBA in easy steps for more help with building your own functions.

Function Structure

The basic form of a function is:

$$NAME\ (Arg1, Arg2, ...)$$

NAME   The function name, always displayed in uppercase

Arg1   The arguments for the function

Arg2

Arguments are separated by commas, but there's no comma after the final argument. The arguments are enclosed by parentheses, which are required even when the function has no arguments – for example, **NOW()**, which returns the current date and time.

We've seen the **SUM** function used with a cell range as arguments but there are other possible arrangements of arguments. There is a requirement for one single argument, but the function can accept optional arguments, with an effectively infinite number supported. The arguments must all be numeric, and may be of these types:

- **Number**   e.g. 100
- **Cell Reference**   e.g. B2
- **Range Reference**   e.g. B4:B8

This is shown in this example worksheet:

The arguments provide the data that the function uses to carry out its calculations.

This example of the **SUM** function illustrates the addition of a number, a cell reference, and a range reference. All of the cells must contain numeric data.

MyBudg...   Michael Price

File | Hom | Inser | Draw | Page | Form | Data | Revie | View | Deve | Help

B10   fx   =SUM(100,B2,B4:B8)

	A	B	C	D	E
1	Budget				
2	Meeting room	200			
3					
4	Transport	250			
5	Telephone	150			
6	Cell Phone	250			
7	Electricity	180			
8	Gas	150			
9					
10	Total	1280			
11	(Including 100				
12	misc expenses)				

Sheet1   +

100%

Typing the Function

Functions are always used in formulas, so you start by typing the equals sign (=). If you'll be using the function on its own, you then type the function name, preferably in lowercase letters – for example, **=sum**.

1 Type an opening parenthesis after the function name

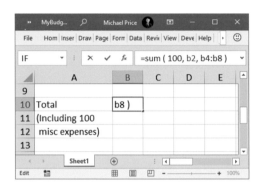

If you put a space before the parenthesis, Excel treats this as an error. For example, if you type **=sum (100,b2,b4:b8)** you get a warning message, with a suggested correction.

2 Type or select each argument – value, cell reference, range reference or defined name for a cell or range reference – then type a closing parenthesis

You must always separate multiple arguments with commas. You can put a space after each comma to make the function expression more readable. Excel ignores these extra spaces.

3 Press **Enter** to complete the formula with the function

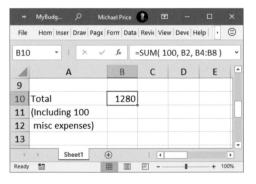

If you mistype the function name (for example, you put **add** instead of **sum**), Excel displays the **#NAME?** error to say the formula contains unrecognized text.

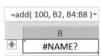

The expression is converted to uppercase, the formula is evaluated, and the result displayed in the cell.

...cont'd

You can use a function as an argument for another function. This is known as **Nesting Functions**. As an example, calculate the average quarterly telephone expenses with a nested **SUM**:

1 Enter **=average(** and then put **sum(a3:c3)**, the first quarter's total, as the first argument

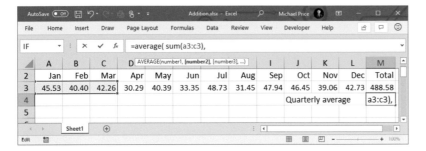

As with any argument, you separate the **SUM** functions with commas, and again you can insert extra spaces to make the components of the formula more evident.

2 Add similar **SUM** expressions for the totals of the other three quarters, as additional arguments

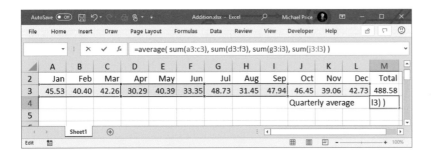

3 Type the closing parenthesis and press **Enter** to complete the interpretation and evaluation of the formula

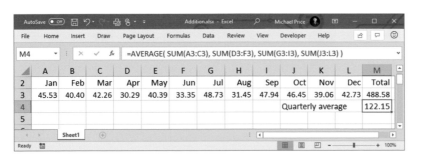

The values of the four **SUM** functions are computed in turn to provide the arguments for the **AVERAGE** function, and then the average itself is computed.

43

AutoComplete

Excel offers the **AutoComplete** feature to assist you with entering function names into a formula. This shows you a list of functions that begin with the same characters you've typed so far.

1 Begin typing a name, and Excel displays a list of the functions that start with the letters you've typed

Excel changes the list of function names as you type more of the name. Select a function name to see a brief description.

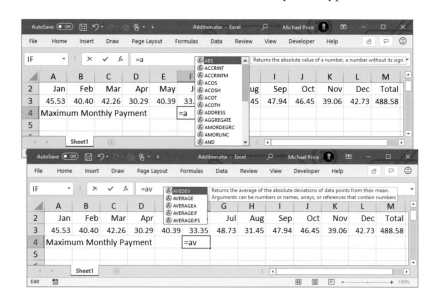

You can click **Tab** to have the selected function inserted into the formula.

2 Continue typing the name to refine the list presented

3 Double-click the required function name to insert that function in the formula

When you've selected the function, Excel displays a pop-up banner showing the function syntax. The current argument is highlighted.

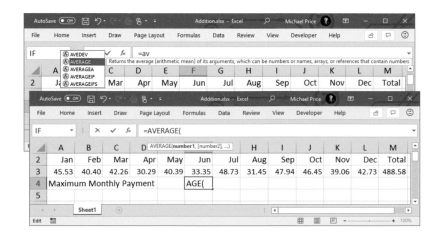

Function Library

If you know the category of function you want, but are not quite sure of the name, you can use the **Function Library** group on the **Formulas** tab. The Ribbon format depends on the current window size, but the same categories are displayed.

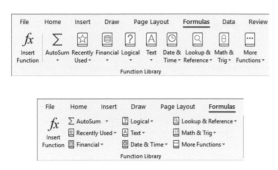

Select the **Formulas** tab and click **More Functions** to see the additional categories that are available.

Statistical	▶
Engineering	▶
Cube	▶
Information	▶
Compatibility	▶
Web	▶

1   When you are at the place in the formula where you need a function, select its category – for example, **Logical**

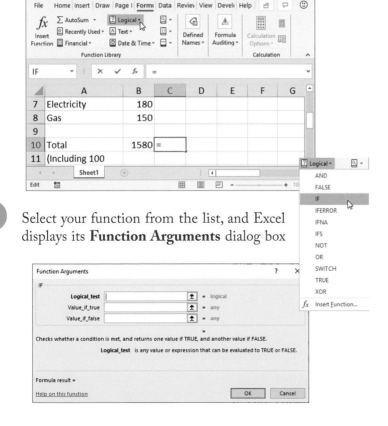

2   Select your function from the list, and Excel displays its **Function Arguments** dialog box

This is where you enter the function's arguments. There's a description of the function, and you can click the **Help on This Function** link to learn more.

...cont'd

3 Enter the arguments for the function into the dialog box, and then click **OK**

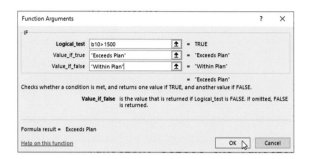

The dialog box indicates how the function behaves with the selected values so you can confirm its actions.

4 Complete the formula and press **Enter** to see the result displayed in the worksheet

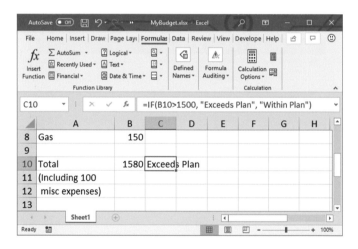

The contents of the **Recently Used** list continually change, and always reflect the latest set of functions that you have accessed.

The **Function Library** group also displays **AutoSum** functions and a list of **Recently Used** functions. These list functions that are likely to be required, and they repeat entries that are found in the individual Function categories.

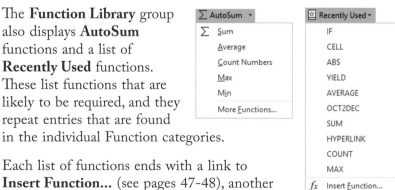

Each list of functions ends with a link to **Insert Function...** (see pages 47-48), another way of selecting the function you require.

Insert Function

There are several links to the **Insert Function** command.

- Select the **Formulas** tab and click **Insert Function** in the **Function Library** group.

- Click the **Insert Function** button on the Formula bar.

- Click the **Insert Function...** or **More Functions...** link, found at the foot of Function category listings.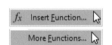

To add a function using the **Insert Function** command, type any preceding part of the formula, then:

1. Invoke **Insert Function** by any of the above methods

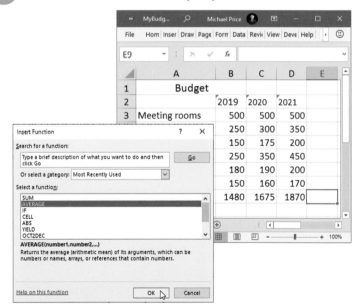

2. The **Insert Function** dialog box appears, with **Most Recently Used** functions listed

3. Select an appropriate Function category, if desired, then select the required function from the list displayed

You could alternatively press key combination **Shift** + **F3** to open the **Insert Function** dialog box.

If you are starting with an empty cell, Excel inserts an **equals sign** (=) when you select the **Insert Function** command, to initiate the formula.

47

The **Insert Function** dialog box lists each of the Function categories (see page 49) and also offers an alphabetic list of **All** functions.

...cont'd

You can use the **Function Arguments** dialog box to modify the arguments for a function in an existing formula. Click the function in the Formula bar and then click the **Insert Function** button.

The **Function Arguments** dialog box is displayed, often with the expected initial argument predefined.

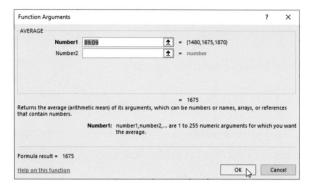

④ Confirm or adjust the arguments then click **OK**

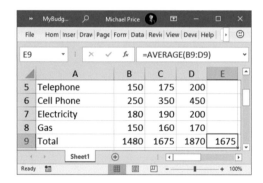

⑤ The formula is completed, and the result is displayed

If you are not certain of the category or function name, you can type a brief description of what you want to do (for example, **Pay Loan**) then click **OK**. The **Insert Function** command will present a list of recommended functions for you to choose from.

If **Insert Function** is unclear about the function you might need, based on the description provided, it will prompt you with **Please rephrase your question**.

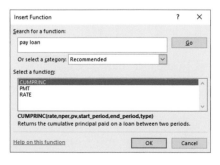

Function Categories

With almost 500 functions included in the latest versions of Excel, some method of organizing them is essential. Excel classifies the functions into Function categories. These are shown in the **Function Library (FL)** group on the **Formulas** tab and in the **Insert Function (IF)** dialog box.

The categories that are used include:

Compatibility	42	
Cube	7	
Database	12	IF only
Date & Time	24	
Engineering	54	
Financial	55	
Information	20	
Logical	11	
Lookup & Reference	19	
Math & Trig	74	
Statistical	110	
Text	28	
Web	3	

The number of functions in each category in the latest version of Excel are shown. Lists that are limited to particular areas are identified.

You will also find listings that duplicate classes of functions, provided under these headings:

All	459	IF only
AutoSum	5	FL only
Recently Used	10	
User Defined		IF only
Euro Currency Tools	3	
Solver Add-in	127	

These extra lists give alternative ways to list or apply functions. They may duplicate entries found in the regular Function categories. The entries displayed may vary, depending on your recent activities.

AutoSum

AutoSum provides complete assistance in inserting commonly used functions. To see it in use for totaling cells:

1 Select the cell adjacent to the range of data to be totaled

You'd select the empty cell to the right of a horizontal range, or immediately below a vertical range.

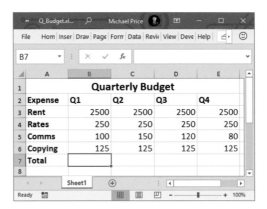

Alternatively, you can select the **Home** tab and click **AutoSum** in the **Editing** group.

2 Select the **Formulas** tab and click **AutoSum** in the **Function Library** group

3 The formula is inserted. Check the range chosen, and press **Enter** to complete the formula

Hot tip

If you select the range itself, the complete function is inserted in the adjacent empty cell. There's not even a need to press **Enter**.

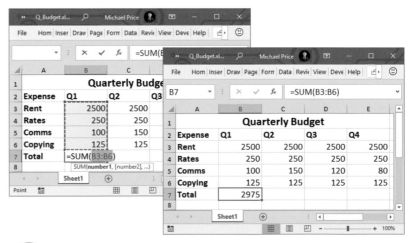

4 Repeat the steps to insert totals for the other quarters

5 Select the empty cell adjacent to the quarterly totals

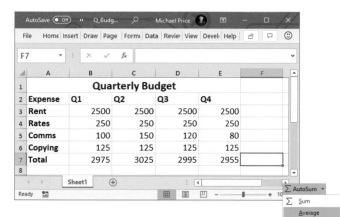

Hot tip

Using **AutoSum**, you can automatically create the formulas for SUM, AVERAGE, COUNT, MIN and MAX functions.

6 Click the arrow on the **AutoSum** button and select the **Average** function

51

7 An **AVERAGE** formula for the selected cells is inserted

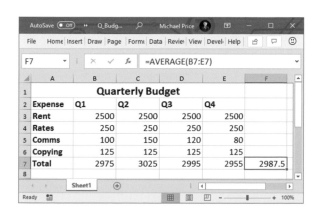

Don't forget

Check the range that has been selected, and press **Enter** to insert the formula.

Recently Used

Excel remembers the 10 most recently used functions and makes them available in several different ways:

1 Select the **Formulas** tab and click **Recently Used** in the **Function Library** group and choose from the list

Whichever way it is loaded, the Recently Used list contains the same functions – the last 10 that were used.

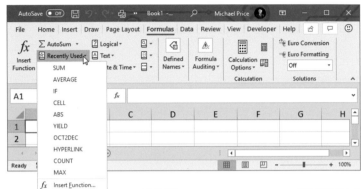

2 Click on the **Insert Function** command (see pages 47-48) and choose the **Most Recently Used** category. Scroll the list to choose the function to re-use

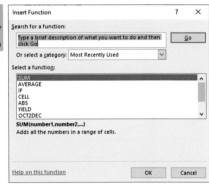

3 Type an **equals sign (=)** to start a formula, and click the arrow on the **Functions** box on the Formula bar

When you start a function the **Name Box** to the left of the Formula bar changes to **Functions** and lists recently used functions.

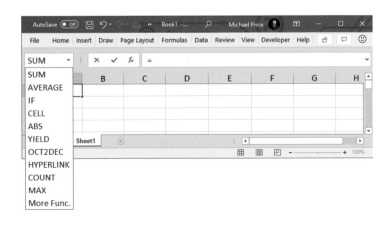

All Functions List

If you know the name (or part of the name) for a function, but are unsure of its category, you can select it from an alphabetic list.

1 Click on the **Insert Function** command and select the category **All** to list all the functions available

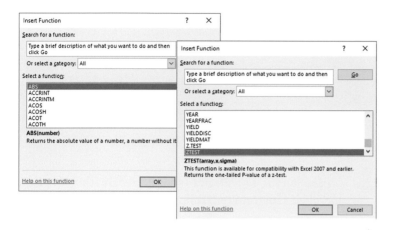

Scroll the list, which runs from **ABS** to **ZTEST**, to locate the function that you want to insert.

You'll also find the alphabetic list on the **Office Support** website.

1 Open **support.office.com/excel,** and scroll down to select the link **List of all Excel functions available**

2 Select the initial letter and scroll down the list to the function you want to insert

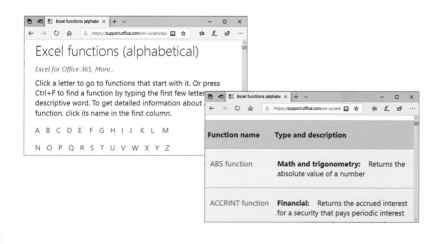

The entry for each function gives a brief description and identifies the category to which it belongs.

Developer Tab

For more advanced use of functions, and to support macros (which you can create to carry out repetitive tasks) you need **Developer** facilities. These are provided on the **Developer** tab, but by default this is not displayed.

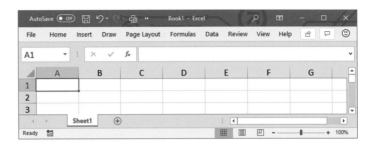

Hot tip

You can right-click the **Tab bar** or the **Title bar** and select **Customize the Ribbon...** to display the appropriate options.

Don't forget

The **Developer** tab will now appear for all worksheets, unless you re-invoke the **Excel Options** and remove the check mark for **Developer**.

1 To display the **Developer** tab, select **File**, then **Options** and click **Customize Ribbon**

2 Click the **Developer** box in the **Main Tabs** section and the **Developer** tab will be added to the Tab bar

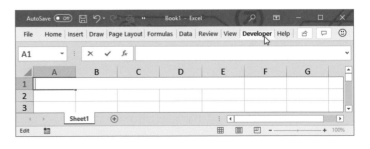

Add-ins

The **Developer** tab provides tools in the **Add-ins** group for installing additional functions.

1 Select the **Add-ins** command to install Office add-ins

2 Click **Office Store** to list the Office add-ins

3 Search for add-ins related to **Excel**, and add any that you wish to try

Hot tip

This process lists add-ins for various Office products but you can search for **Excel** to limit the display to Excel-related add-ins.

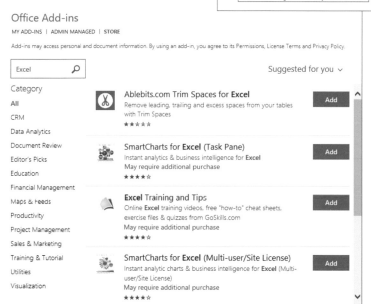

4 Select the **Excel Add-ins** command for add-ins available with Excel

5 Click the box for the Excel add-ins you want then click **OK** to activate them

Don't forget

Some add-ins are included in the Excel installation, but they are not initially activated.

...cont'd

6 Select the **COM Add-ins** command to list the aids for developers to automate Excel tasks

The **Developer** tab also includes the **Code** group with tools for using **Visual Basic** and creating **macros**.

7 Click the box for the **COM** add-ins you want then click **OK** to make them available

You can also manage add-ins from within **Excel Options**:

1 Select the **File** tab, click **Options** and select **Add-ins**

2 Review the current status of your system

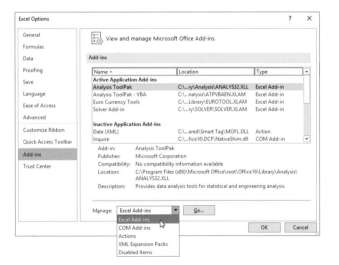

When you select **Go**, you are presented with the same options for activating add-ins that you receive via the **Developer** tab.

3 Select the type of add-ins you want to manage and click **Go** to invoke the facility to activate or deactivate specific add-ins of that type on your system

4

Math & Trig and Logical

The first sets of Function categories presented are the Math & Trig category and the Logical category. The functions contained in these categories are discussed. Examples of the use of some of these functions are given.

Math & Trig Category

The 74 functions in the Excel Math & Trig category perform many of the common mathematical calculations, extending the facilities provided by the basic mathematical operators provided for creating formulas (see pages 14-15). They include functions in the following areas:

- Numeric Information
- Mathematical Operations
- Rounding
- Matrix
- Random Numbers
- Conditional Sums
- Exponents
- Logarithms
- Factorials
- Trigonometry

There are two ways to see the complete list of Math & Trig functions:

Operations supported by these functions range from sums and products to logarithms, factorials and random numbers.

With 74 functions, this is the largest of the main categories in the **Function Library**.

Select any entry in the list to display its **Function Arguments** dialog box, which includes a description of the function's operation.

1 Select the **Formulas** tab and click the **Math & Trig** category in the **Function Library** group

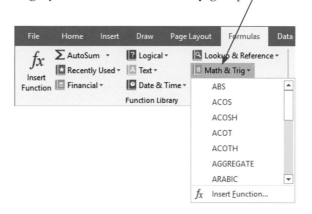

Scroll the list to review the Math & Trig functions, displayed alphabetically, and choose the one you need

...cont'd

2 Alternatively, choose the **Insert Function** command and select the category **Math & Trig**

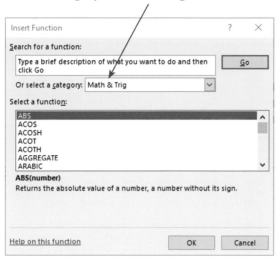

There are several ways of selecting the Insert Function command (see pages 47-48). Each displays the **Insert Function** dialog box and gives access to the **Select a Category** option.

In the Math & Trig list produced by either method you will find 74 functions, of which 25 are Trig functions (see pages 64-65).

ABS	CSC	MULTINOMIAL	SQRT
ACOS	CSCH	MUNIT	SQRTPI
ACOSH	DECIMAL	ODD	SUBTOTAL
ACOT	DEGREES	PI	SUM
ACOTH	EVEN	POWER	SUMIF
AGGREGATE	EXP	PRODUCT	SUMIFS
ARABIC	FACT	QUOTIENT	SUMPRODUCT
ASIN	FACTDOUBLE	RADIANS	SUMSQ
ASINH	FLOOR.MATH	RAND	SUMX2MY2
ATAN	GCD	RANDBETWEEN	SUMX2PY2
ATAN2	INT	ROMAN	SUMXMY2
ATANH	LCM	ROUND	TAN
BASE	LN	ROUNDDOWN	TANH
CEILING.MATH	LOG	ROUNDUP	TRUNC
COMBIN	LOG10	SEC	
COMBINA	MDETERM	SECH	
COS	MINVERSE	SERIESSUM	
COSH	MMULT	SIGN	
COT	MOD	SIN	
COTH	MROUND	SINH	

You'll also find Math functions that belong to earlier versions of Excel, in the **Compatibility** category. These have been superseded by newer functions, but are retained to support older worksheets.

There are additional Math functions to be found in the Statistical category and the Engineering category.

Sum Functions

Perhaps the most used Excel function is **SUM**. This totals numbers, cells and ranges of cells. For example, in this sales commission worksheet, the total sales for an individual salesman are calculated as **=SUM(B3:E3)**.

Hot tip

In this example, the range **B3:E3** contains the quarterly sales data for the first salesman, with subsequent sales data in **B4:E4** etc.

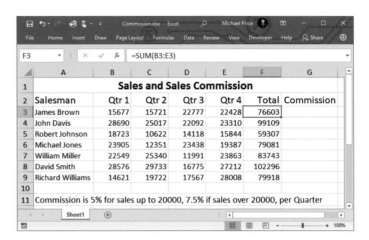

However, additions are not always so simple. Suppose you want to calculate commission for a salesman, where sales up to 20,000 per quarter earn 5%, while sales that exceed 20,000 earn 7.5%.

1 To calculate commission on quarterly sales up to 20,000 you could enter **=SUMIF(B3:E3, "<=20000")*5%**

Don't forget

SUMIF adds only those cells that meet the criteria specified, in this case values up to and including 20,000. The total is then multiplied by the commission rate.

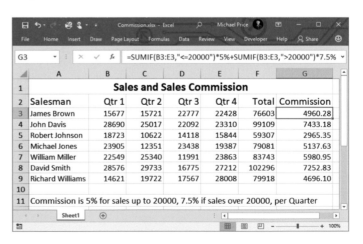

2 Add the commission for sales exceeding 20,000 with **+SUMIF(B3:E3,">20000")*7.5%**

Random Numbers

The data for the example sales commission worksheet was created using one of the random number functions.

1 Select the first date cell **B3** and enter the formula
=RANDBETWEEN(10000,30000)

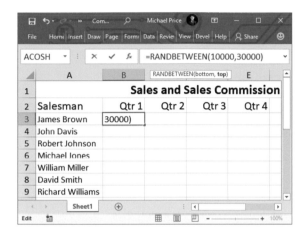

Hot tip

Numbers between 10,000 and 30,000 will make a realistic sample worksheet for the purposes of demonstrating Math functions.

2 Copy the cell to the Clipboard with shortcut key **Ctrl + C**

3 Select all the sales data cells **B3:E9** and **Paste** using shortcut key **Ctrl + V** to insert the formula in all the cells

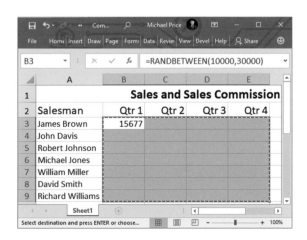

Don't forget

Random numbers between the values specified will be generated in each of the data cells.

The random numbers will be regenerated whenever the worksheet is recalculated, so it is necessary to replace the formulas by the actual numeric values initially created.

...cont'd

Don't forget

Using **Copy** then **Paste Values** ensures that the actual values rather than the formulas are stored in the cells.

4 Select data cells **B3:E9** and **Copy** them to the Clipboard using shortcut key **Ctrl + C**

5 Select the **Home** tab and click **Paste**, **Paste Values** to replace the formulas with their current values

The data values will now remain fixed whenever the worksheet is recalculated.

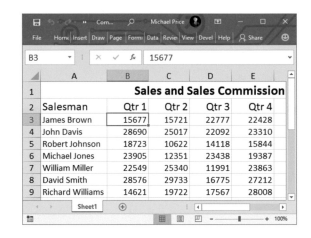

There is another random number function called RAND that requires no arguments and produces random decimal numbers between 0 and 1.

1 Type **=RAND( )** and press **Enter**

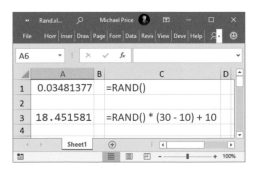

2 To create a random number between two numbers – say, 10 and 30 – you'd type **=RAND() * (30 - 10) + 10**

Hot tip

At the time of writing, Microsoft is previewing a new function called **RANDARRAY** that generates an array of random numbers between 0 and 1, or between two specified numbers, where you can request decimals or whole numbers.

Rounding Functions

Another frequently required capability in worksheets is **Rounding**. The Math functions list includes 10 such functions:

- CEILING.MATH
- FLOOR.MATH
- MROUND
- ROUND
- ROUNDUP

- EVEN
- INT
- ODD
- ROUNDDOWN
- TRUNC

The following worksheet illustrates some of these functions being applied to positive and negative numbers.

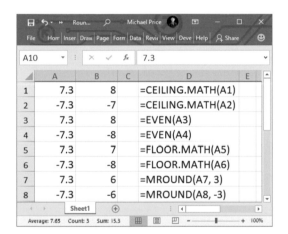

There are some additional Rounding functions, not included in the list of Math functions, provided for compatibility purposes:

- CEILING
- CEILING.PRECISE
- FLOOR
- FLOOR.PRECISE
- ISO.CEILING

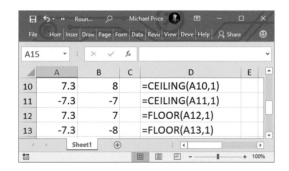

63

Trig Functions

Most of the Trig functions will be familiar to anyone who has studied mathematics, being related to Sine, Cosine, Tangent, etc. These functions include:

ACOS • ACOSH • ACOT • ACOTH • ASIN
ASINH • ATAN • ATAN2 • ATANH • COS
COSH • COT • COTH • CSC • CSCH • SEC
SECH • SIN • SINH • TAN • TANH

In addition, there are Trig functions associated with the value Pi:

PI • SQRTPI

Finally, there are functions that convert the values of angles between radians and degrees:

DEGREES • RADIANS

You can apply Trig functions to calculate the distance between two places (New York City and Paris, for example) using their latitude and longitude co-ordinates.

These co-ordinates are usually expressed in degrees, but you can convert them to radians using the associated function.

 Enter **=RADIANS(B3)**, where **B3** contains the latitude for the first location

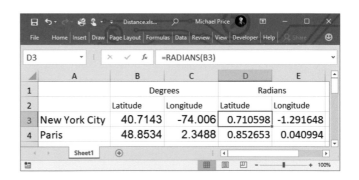

	Degrees		Radians	
	Latitude	Longitude	Latitude	Longitude
New York City	40.7143	-74.006	0.710598	-1.291648
Paris	48.8534	2.3488	0.852653	0.040994

2 Copy the formula to convert the remaining co-ordinates from **degrees** to **radians**

The converted co-ordinates can now be used to calculate the distance between the locations.

All of these functions accept arguments in the form of angles expressed in **radians**.

Latitude and longitude may also be expressed in the form of **degrees(°), minutes('), seconds('')**.

New York City is:
40°42'51.4'' N
74°0'21.5'' W
Paris is:
48°51'12.28'' N
2°20'55.68'' W

Divide by 60 to convert **seconds** to **minutes**. Divide by 60 to convert **minutes** to **degrees**.

There's a standard formula to calculate the distance between two co-ordinates, where these are expressed in **radians**:

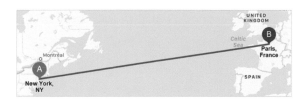

The value in cell **C8** is the radius of the Earth, expressed in **miles**. Since the Earth is not a perfect sphere, the result will be approximate.

1 Enter **=ACOS(SIN(D3)*SIN(D4)+COS(D3)*COS(D4) *COS(E4-E3))*C8** to calculate the distance in miles

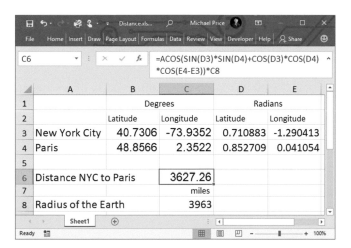

2 Similarly, you can calculate the distance between places in **nautical miles** or in **kilometers**

The values in cells **D8** and **E8** are the radius of the Earth, expressed in **nautical miles** and **kilometers** respectively.

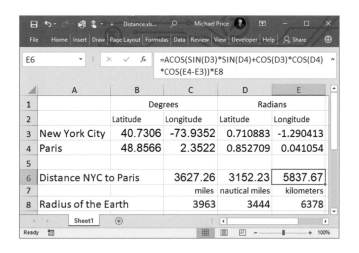

Logical Category

The Logical functions in Excel allow you to investigate values and expressions, and take action based on the results. This provides the basis for decision-making capabilities in your worksheets. There are just 11 of these functions, but they form perhaps the most powerful part of Excel.

The Logical functions divide into several groups:

Boolean Operators

AND	Tests a set of conditions and returns **True** if **All** of the conditions evaluate to True, or **False** otherwise.
OR	Tests a set of conditions and returns **True** if **Any** of the conditions evaluate to True, or **False** otherwise.
XOR	Returns a logical **Exclusive Or** of all arguments.
NOT	Returns the opposite logical value of a supplied logical value or expression.

Constant Values

TRUE	Returns the logical value **True**.
FALSE	Returns the logical value **False**.

Conditional Analysis

IF	Tests a condition and returns one result if the condition is **True**, and another result if the condition is **False**.
IFERROR	Tests if a value or expression returns an error, and if so, returns a specified value.
IFNA	Tests if an expression returns a **#N/A** error and if so, returns an alternative specified value.
IFS	Tests a set of conditions and returns the first condition that evaluates to **True**.
SWITCH	Compares a number of values to a test expression and returns the first value that matches.

While Excel can't make decisions for you, it can carry out checks on the values and expressions you specify, to put you in the position where you can choose the appropriate action.

The **IFS** and the **SWITCH** functions were both added to Excel 2019 and so are not available in previous releases.

IF Function

Imagine you need to display the commission rates earned each quarter, for the salesmen in the worksheet discussed on page 60.

1 Copy the headings and salesmen names

Salesman	Qtr 1	Qtr 2	Qtr 3	Qtr 4
Commission Rates Earned				
James Brown	"7.5%")			
John Davis				
Robert Johnson				
Michael Jones				
William Miller				
David Smith				
Richard Williams				

Formula bar: `=IF(B3<=20000, "5%", "7.5%")`

2 Select the data cell for the first salesman, first quarter and enter **=IF(B3<=20000), "5%", "7.5%")**

If the condition is **True**, then the second argument is displayed. If the condition is **False**, then the third argument is displayed.

3 Copy the formula into the data cells for all the salesmen and each of the quarters

Formula bar: `=IF(E9<=20000, "5%", "7.5%")`

Salesman	Qtr 1	Qtr 2	Qtr 3	Qtr 4
Commission Rates Earned				
James Brown	5%	5%	7.5%	7.5%
John Davis	7.5%	7.5%	7.5%	7.5%
Robert Johnson	5%	5%	5%	5%
Michael Jones	7.5%	5%	7.5%	5%
William Miller	7.5%	7.5%	5%	7.5%
David Smith	7.5%	7.5%	5%	7.5%
Richard Williams	5%	5%	5%	7.5%

You'll see the rate earned by each salesman for each quarter, either 5% or 7.5% depending on the sales value.

...cont'd

Suppose there were more than two levels of commission; for example: 5% up to 15,000, 6% up to 20,000, 7% up to 25,000 and 8% over 25,000. To test multiple conditions, you could nest **IF** functions in place of the **FALSE** value.

1 Select the first data cell and enter **=IF(B3<=15000, "5%",IF(B3<=20000,"6%",IF(B3<=25000,"7%","8%")))**

There's one final closing parentheses for each of the **IF** functions.

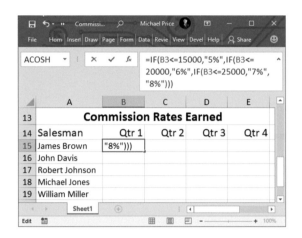

2 Copy the formula into the data cells for all the salesmen and each of the quarters

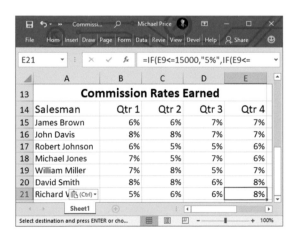

You'll see the rate earned by each salesman for each quarter, being 5%, 6%, 7% or 8%, depending on the sales value.

IFS Function

Another way to test multiple conditions is with the **IFS** function, which is new in Excel 2019. This function returns the value associated with the first condition found to be **TRUE**. It avoids the need for nested **IFS**, and gives a shorter, easier to read formula.

1 In the first data cell type **=IFS(B3<=15000,"5%", B3<=20000,"6%",B3<=25000,"7%",B3>25000,"8%")**

The function contains pairs of conditions and values, and there's just a single pair of parentheses.

Hot tip

Each condition in the **IFS** function is tested in turn, until a **TRUE** result is found and the associated value is displayed.

	A	B	C	D	E
13	**Commission Rates Earned**				
14	Salesman	Qtr 1	Qtr 2	Qtr 3	Qtr 4
15	James Brown	,"8%")			
16	John Davis				
17	Robert Johnson				
18	Michael Jones				
19	William Miller				

Formula bar: =IFS(B3<=15000,"5%",B3<=20000,"6%",B3<=25000,"7%",B3>25000,"8%")

2 Copy the formula into the data cells for all the salesmen and each of the quarters

Don't forget

All conditions in the **IFS** function must return **TRUE** or **FALSE** results, and there must always be at least one **TRUE** result, or a **#N/A** error will be displayed.

Formula bar: =IFS(E9<=15000,"5%",E9<=

	A	B	C	D	E
13	**Commission Rates Earned**				
14	Salesman	Qtr 1	Qtr 2	Qtr 3	Qtr 4
15	James Brown	6%	6%	7%	7%
16	John Davis	8%	8%	7%	7%
17	Robert Johnson	6%	5%	5%	6%
18	Michael Jones	7%	5%	7%	6%
19	William Miller	7%	8%	5%	7%
20	David Smith	8%	8%	6%	8%
21	Richard V	5%	6%	6%	8%

You'll see the rate earned by each salesman for each quarter, appropriate to the particular sales value.

SWITCH Function

The **SWITCH** function evaluates an expression and compares the result to a list of values, each with an associated result. It returns the result corresponding to the first matching value. If there is no match, an optional default value may be returned.

Hot tip

The **SWITCH** function is a simpler alternative to **IFS** and nested **IF** functions, since it only needs a single expression.

1 Enter a date, for example **12/25/2000**, in cell **B2**

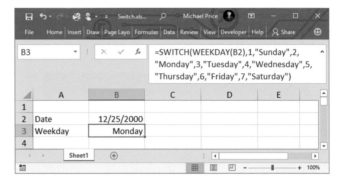

Hot tip

Note that if no match is found (and no default value for mismatch is provided) the function returns the **#N/A** error indicator.

2 Type the formula **=SWITCH(WEEKDAY(B2),1, "Sunday",2, "Monday",3,"Tuesday",4,"Wednesday",5, "Thursday",6,"Friday",7,"Saturday")** in cell **B3**

When this formula is evaluated, it displays the day of the week.

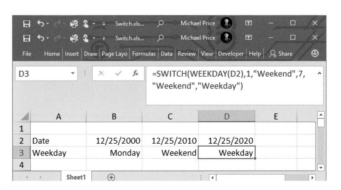

Hot tip

You can specify a default value to be displayed if there is no match between the expression and the specified values.

3 Formula **=SWITCH(WEEKDAY(B2),1,"Weekend",7, "Weekend","Weekday")** displays **Weekend** for the days 1 or 7, and **Weekday** for other days

5 Date & Time and Text

Here we investigate the Function categories of Date & Time and Text. The functions contained in these categories are discussed and relevant issues raised. Examples of the use of some of the functions in each category are presented.

Date & Time Category

Select **Formulas,** then **Date & Time** from the Functions Library group and you'll see a list of 24 functions, including:

DATE • DATEVALUE • DAY • DAYS • DAYS360
EDATE • EOMONTH • HOUR • ISOWEEKNUM
MINUTE • MONTH • NETWORKDAYS
NETWORKDAYS.INTL • NOW • SECOND • TIME
TIMEVALUE • TODAY • WEEKDAY • WEEKNUM
WORKDAY • WORKDAY.INTL • YEAR • YEARFRAC

All these functions work with dates and times stored as serial numbers, although formatting is used to present the date and time values in a variety of styles (see pages 73-74). Here the General format is applied to the cells containing dates, so you can see the underlying serial number. Dates start from January 1, 1900, which is serial number 1.

The integer part of the serial number represents the day, and the decimal part is the time.

Hot tip

Workbooks created in Excel 2008 for Mac and earlier have dates starting from January 2, 1904. If you have received such a workbook, you can select **File**, **Options**, **Advanced** and choose Use **1904 date system** for that workbook.

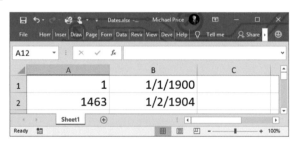

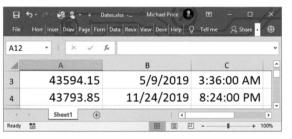

The latest date that you can set in Excel is December 31 of the year 9999.

Beware

12/31/9999 is the latest date supported by Excel, in either the 1900 date system or the 1904 date system.

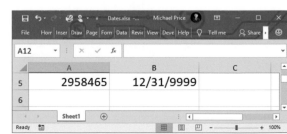

Date Formats

Although the date is simply a serial number, Excel provides many different formats for displaying the date.

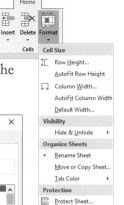

1 Select the **Home** tab, click **Format** in the Cells group and select **Format Cells...**

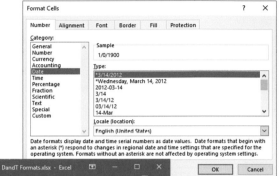

For a quick way to open the Format Cells dialog box, press the **Ctrl + 1** shortcut keys.

2 Select **Date** and choose one of the 18 formats offered

3 Click **OK** to apply the selected format

You can display the whole date or portions of the date in a variety of ways.

Some formats also display the Time component of the Date value – the decimal part of the serial number.

Choose the location to see date formats that are particular to the selected region.

You could select Format Cells, Custom and design your own special formats for Date.

Time Formats

Time is the decimal portion of a Date serial number or, for Time on its own, a decimal serial number that is between 0 and 1.

As with Date, Excel provides a number of different ways of displaying time.

1 Open the **Format Cells** dialog box

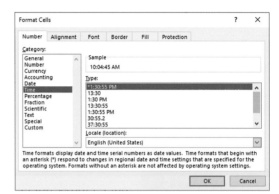

2 Select **Time** and choose one of the nine formats offered

You can choose formats that display or hide the Seconds component or the Hours component and use the 24-hour clock, or display an AM or PM suffix.

The non-decimal part of the serial number contains the associated date, and two of the formats display the combined date and time values, in the 12-hour AM/PM style, or the 24-hour style.

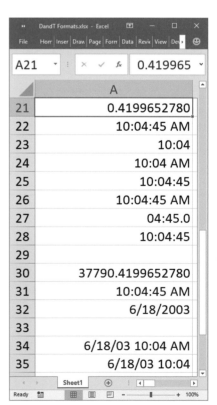

Leap Year Inconsistency

Excel for Windows has a deliberate inconsistency, in that it assumes 1900 is a leap year and serial number 60 is February 29, 1900. This was done to match the Lotus 123 spreadsheet program, which had the same assumption built in.

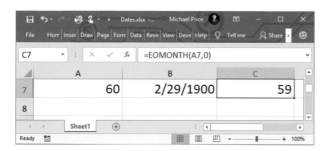

Despite this built-in inconsistency, the **EOMONTH** function correctly specifies 59 as the serial number for the end of February 1900.

As a consequence, weekdays before March 1, 1900 are ill-defined.

For example, Excel defines January 1, 1900 as a Sunday, as you'll see if you apply the **WEEKDAY** function to serial number 1.

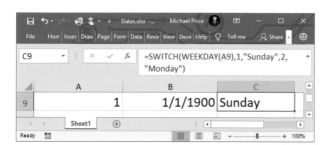

However, January 1, 1900 was actually a Monday, as confirmed by the website **www.dayoftheweek.org**

Dates from March 1, 1900 onward are identified correctly. Workbooks using the 1904 date system suffer no inconsistency.

Excel also miscounts the number of days between two dates, if the first date is February 28, 1900 or earlier, and the second is March 1, 1900 or later.

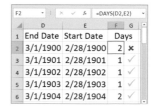

1900 is incorrectly treated as a leap year. 1904 is correctly treated as such.

DATEDIF Function

Although not listed as one of the current Time & Date functions, the **DATEDIF** function is included in Excel. It is provided for backward compatibility with older Lotus 123 workbooks.

It is not fully documented and Excel does not prompt with the list or arguments when you enter the function name.

The function has three required arguments and the syntax is:

=DATEDIF (Start_date, End_date, Unit)

The start and end dates may be entered as text strings within quotation marks, as serial numbers, as results of other formulas or functions (for example, **DATEVALUE** or **TODAY**), or as references to cells containing such values.

Unit is a text code indicating the unit of time, and you can have the following six options:

"y"	Difference in complete years
"m"	Difference in complete months
"d"	Difference in days
"md"	Difference in days, ignoring months and years
"ym"	Difference in months, ignoring days and years
"yd"	Difference in days, ignoring years

Here are some examples of the **DATEDIF** function in use.

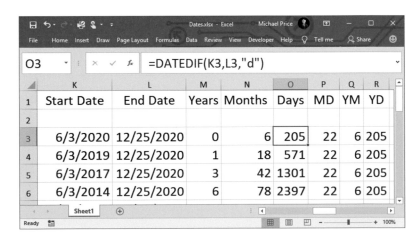

These illustrate the results provided by each of the six units with various start and end date combinations.

Hot tip

If the Start Date is greater than the End Date, the function returns a #NUM! error.

10/12/2010	8/30/2010	#NUM!

Beware

DATEDIF is known to have problems with the "md" option, which can give erroneous results in some circumstances. This option should therefore be used with caution.

Don't forget

The quotation marks around the unit are required. However, the unit may be entered in uppercase or lowercase with no effect on the result displayed.

=DATEDIF(K3,L3,"d")

	K	L	M	N	O	P	Q	R
1	Start Date	End Date	Years	Months	Days	MD	YM	YD
2								
3	6/3/2020	12/25/2020	0	6	205	22	6	205
4	6/3/2019	12/25/2020	1	18	571	22	6	205
5	6/3/2017	12/25/2020	3	42	1301	22	6	205
6	6/3/2014	12/25/2020	6	78	2397	22	6	205

Calculating the age of a person is a surprisingly complex task in Excel. However, the **DATEDIF** function provides help with this. To get the age in whole years, you use the "y" unit.

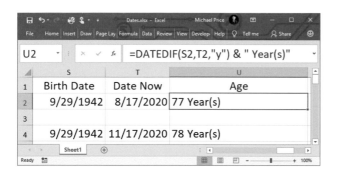

To get the age in years, months and days, you use an instance of the **DATEDIF** function to calculate each component.

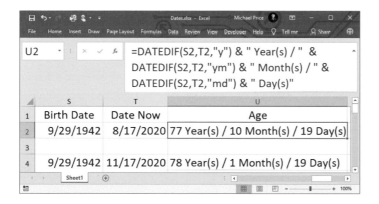

The "y" unit gives the years, the "ym" unit gives the months, and the "md" unit gives the days.

An alternative method would be to use the separate functions **YEAR**, **MONTH** and **DAY**.

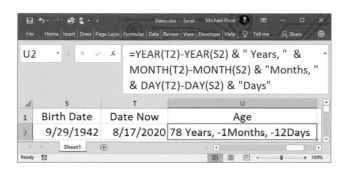

Workday Functions

The **NETWORKDAYS** function returns the number of whole working days between the StartDate and the EndDate.

The syntax of this function is:

NETWORKDAYS(StartDate, EndDate, [Holidays])

Working days exclude weekends, assumed to be Saturday and Sunday, and any dates identified in the optional argument Holidays (a range of cells).

In this example, there are 155 in the project period shown, with 22 weekends and 3 holidays, leaving a total of 108 workdays.

Don't forget

Dates should be defined as serial numbers since problems can arise with dates entered as text.

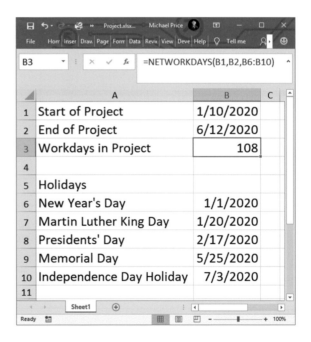

If your project has a different work pattern, you may need to use the other Workday function **NETWORKDAYS.INTL**, which allows you to specify which days are non-working days.

This function has the syntax:

NETWORKDAYS.INTL(StartDate, EndDate, [Weekend] [Holidays])

There is an additional optional argument: Weekend. This contains a weekend number or string that specifies which days are to be treated as non-working days.

Hot tip

If the Start Date is later than the End Date, in either function, a negative value is returned.

78

The Weekend numbers are 1-7 or 11-17 and have the following interpretations:

1 Saturday, Sunday	11 Sunday only
2 Sunday, Monday	12 Monday only
3 Monday, Tuesday	13 Tuesday only
4 Tuesday, Wednesday	14 Wednesday only
5 Wednesday, Thursday	15 Thursday only
6 Thursday, Friday	16 Friday only
7 Friday, Saturday	17 Saturday only

For other than a one- or two-day weekend, you'd specify the Weekend string. This is seven characters long, with each character representing a day of the week, starting with Monday and ending with Sunday. In this string, 1 represents a non-workday and 0 represents a workday. Note that only the characters 1 and 0 are permitted in the Weekend string.

For example, to specify a three-day weekend, Saturday to Monday, and a four-day work week, Tuesday to Friday, you'd use the Weekend string "1000011".

When the Weekend argument is omitted, the default value of 1 (Saturday, Sunday) is assumed.

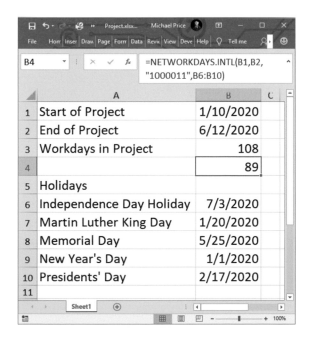

`=NETWORKDAYS.INTL(B1,B2,"1000011",B6:B10)`

	A	B
1	Start of Project	1/10/2020
2	End of Project	6/12/2020
3	Workdays in Project	108
4		89
5	Holidays	
6	Independence Day Holiday	7/3/2020
7	Martin Luther King Day	1/20/2020
8	Memorial Day	5/25/2020
9	New Year's Day	1/1/2020
10	Presidents' Day	2/17/2020

It doesn't matter what sequence the list of holidays is in – the relevant holidays for the project period are dropped from the total number of workdays.

Text Category

When you select Formulas, then Text from the Functions Library group, you'll see a list of 28 functions, including:

BAHTTEXT • CHAR • CLEAN • CODE • CONCAT
DOLLAR • EXACT • FIND • FIXED • LEFT • LEN
LOWER • MID • NUMBERVALUE • PROPER
REPLACE • REPT • RIGHT • SEARCH,
SUBSTITUTE • T • TEXT • TEXTJOIN • TRIM,
UNICHAR • UNICODE • UPPER • VALUE

There are additional Text functions that are designed for the DBCS languages:

AS • DBCS • PHONETIC

There are also DBCS versions of the functions FIND, LEN, MID, REPLACE, RIGHT, SEARCH (with B added to the function name).

Text functions work with strings, which are group of characters used as data. They may contain words, letters, numbers, spaces, symbols and special characters. By default, text strings are left-aligned in a cell while number data is aligned to the right.

If you type letters or a mixture of letters and numbers, Excel treats the value as a string. The cell is given the General format. If you enter numbers alone, Excel will treat this as a number value. If it is meant to be a string value, there are two ways to ensure this:

1 Precede the number with an apostrophe ('), or format the cell as text

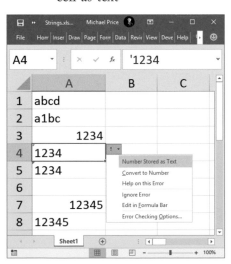

The number you enter will be left-aligned and stored as text.

If you have previously entered a number into a cell, and it has been treated as a number value, you can change the cell format to Text. The value will then be displayed as text (with no warning message indication).

Hot tip

The DBCS (Double Byte Character Set) languages are Chinese (Simplified), Chinese (Traditional), Japanese and Korean.

Don't forget

With either method of entering text, the cell is flagged with a warning message indicating Number Stored as Text.

CONCAT Function

The **CONCAT** function combines text from multiple ranges and/ or strings. It supersedes the **CONCATENATE** function, which deals with strings only, not arrays.

CONCAT doesn't provide a delimiter and there's no option to ignore empty arguments. There must be at least one argument, with a maximum of 253 arguments. Each can be a reference to a cell with a string, or to a range of cells defining an array of strings.

1 Enter **=CONCAT(E1:F5,H1:I5,K1:K5,M1)**, specifying arrays and string

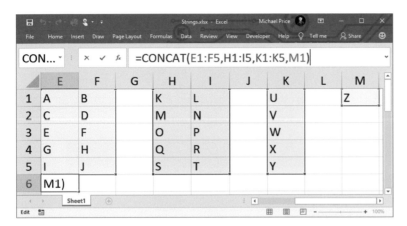

2 The arrays and the string are combined

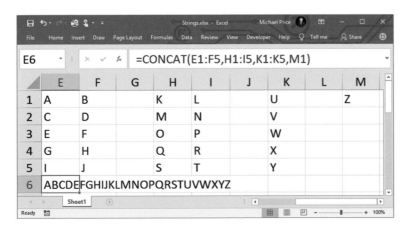

Note that the cells in an array of strings are joined together, row by row, then the next array or string is attached.

Hot tip

To include a delimiter between the text items and to remove empty arguments, you can use the TEXTJOIN function (see page 82).

Beware

If the resulting string exceeds 32767 characters (cell limit), the CONCAT function returns a #VALUE! error.

With an empty string as Delimiter, and False for Ignore_Empty as an empty text string, this function will act just like CONCAT.

The Delimiter can be an array of strings, each of which would be used in turn, repeating the set as needed.

The result may have a warning message saying: Formula Refers to Empty Cells.

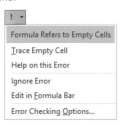

TEXTJOIN Function

The **TEXTJOIN** function combines the text from multiple ranges and/or strings, and includes a delimiter you specify between each text value that will be combined.

There are three required arguments:

Delimiter   A text string, either empty or with one or more characters, enclosed by double quotes, or a reference to a valid text string. If a number is supplied, it will be treated as text.

Ignore_Empty If TRUE, empty cells are ignored.

Text1   First text item.

There can be additional text items to be joined, separated by the delimiter, with a maximum of 251 such items.

Each text item can be a text string, or a reference to a text string, or an array of strings (e.g. a range of cells).

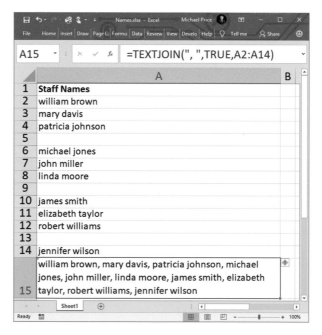

If appropriate, you can use the **PROPER** function to change all the initial letters of the words into uppercase, and convert all the other letters into lowercase.

William Brown, Mary Davis, Patricia Johnson, Michael Jones, John Miller, Linda Moore, James Smith, Elizabeth Taylor, Robert Williams, Jennifer Wilson

Case Functions

We've seen that the **PROPER** function capitalizes the first letter of all the words in a text string.

1 With a mixed case string in cell B1, enter the formula **=PROPER(B1)**

There are two other functions that change the case of text. These are the **UPPER** and **LOWER** functions. Like the **PROPER** function, these functions have a single argument – the text string to be converted or, more usually, a reference to that text string.

2 Enter the formula **=UPPER(B1)**

3 Enter the formula **=LOWER(B1)**

The **PROPER** function effectively converts the text string into a **Title** format, with all the words capitalized.

Excel has just three functions that can change the case of text in a string, while Microsoft Word features five such functions.

Sentence Case

You may wish to convert your text string into sentence case, where the first letter of the first word is capitalized. Unfortunately, Excel lacks the function to carry out this conversion. But you can create a formula to complete this task.

Hot tip

This takes the first character on the left of the string and converts it to uppercase, then takes all the characters except the first and converts them to lowercase, then joins the two components.

1 Enter the following formula
**=CONCAT(UPPER(LEFT(B1,1)),
LOWER(RIGHT(B1,(LEN(B1)-1))))**

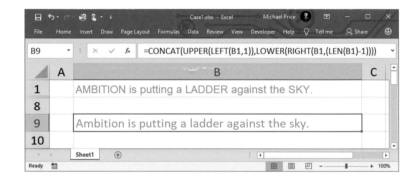

With more than one sentence in the text in the cell, you'll need a different formula. For example:

Hot tip

This converts the whole string to lowercase. It then replaces each full stop plus blank with a unique string with a number ("zzz9"). Then, all remaining blanks are replaced by a unique string ("xxxx"). Each sentence is now effectively a word separated by a number. **PROPER** will capitalize these words. Then, the full stops and the blanks are restored. The text is now in sentence case.

2 Enter the formula:
**SUBSTITUTE(SUBSTITUTE(PROPER(
SUBSTITUTE(SUBSTITUTE(LOWER(B11),".
 ","zzz9")," ","xxxx")),"zzz9",". "),"xxxx"," ")**

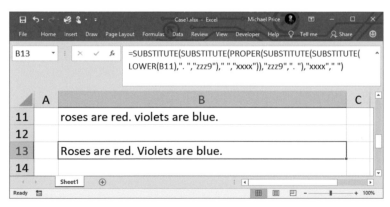

If your text contains question marks (?) you'd have to incorporate checks for that character as well. Similarly, you might need to check for exclamation marks (!).

SUBSTITUTE Function

In the formula to convert multiple sentences to sentence case, the **SUBSTITUTE** function was used. This function substitutes NewText for OldText in the Text string. You use this function when you want to exchange specific text in the Text string.

There are three required arguments and one optional argument:

SUBSTITUTE(Text, OldText, NewText, [InstanceNum])

Text   The text string, or a reference to the relevant cell.
OldText   The text you want to exchange.
NewText   The text you want to place in the string.
InstanceNum   The occurrence of OldText you want to exchange.

You'd use the **REPLACE** function when you want to exchange any text that occurs in a specific location in the Text.

If you are sent spreadsheets from another country, you may find they use different separators for thousands and decimals.

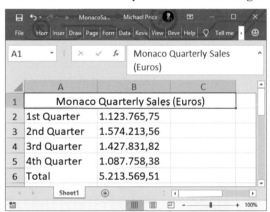

If you provide the InstanceNum argument, only that instance of OldText is exchanged. Otherwise, all instances are exchanged.

1   **SUBSTITUTE** a null character for the "." thousands separator, then **SUBSTITUTE** "." for the "," decimal separator, then apply the **VALUE** function to convert the result to a number, with default thousands and decimal separators

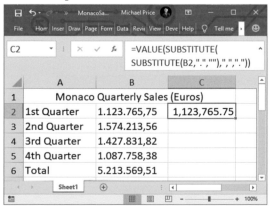

Copy the formula to exchange the separators for the remaining numbers.

| 1,123,765.75 |
| 1,574,213.56 |
| 1,427,831.82 |
| 1,087,758.38 |
| 5,213,569.51 |

BAHTTEXT Function

This function converts a number to Thai text and adds a suffix of "Baht" to the whole number and "Satang" to the decimal part.

The syntax is straightforward:

BAHTTEXT(number)

There is just one required argument: Number, which is the number to be converted to text, or a reference to a cell containing that number, or a formula that evaluates to that number.

Here are some examples that illustrate the results:

Baht is the official currency of Thailand. This is the only currency and Thai is the only language for which Excel provides a function expressing numbers in words.

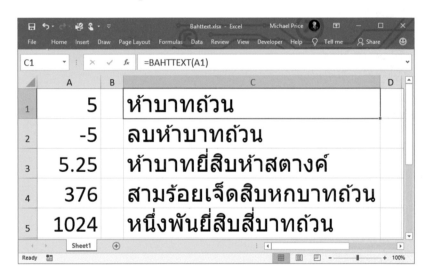

This is the only function in Excel that converts numbers to words. There's no function, for example, to display numbers as English words. However, you can add this capability using **SPELLNUMBER**. This is a User Defined Function (UDF) that lets you convert a number to its equivalent dollar and cent amount in words. The code for this is provided in the Microsoft Office Support website. As an example:

You may find other versions of **SPELLNUMBER** on the internet that convert numbers to words using other currencies (or with no currency specified).

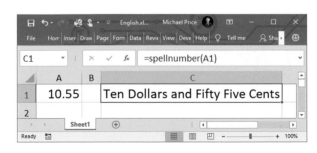

6 Financial and Statistical

Now we review two more Function categories: Financial and Statistical. The functions contained in these categories are discussed, and examples of the use of some of the functions in each category are included.

Financial Category

There are 55 functions in the Financial category. These include functions for:

- Coupon Date
- Depreciation and Amortization
- Dollar Conversion
- Interest Rate Conversion
- Security
- Series of Non-Periodic Variable Cash Flows
- Series of Periodic Constant Cash Flows
- Single Cash Flow
- Treasury Bill

To see a full list of the Financial functions:

Don't forget

Select **Formulas** and click **Financial** to see a simple list of all the functions. Move the mouse pointer over an entry to see the arguments it uses and a description.

1 Select **Formulas**, click the **Insert Function** button and select the **Financial** category

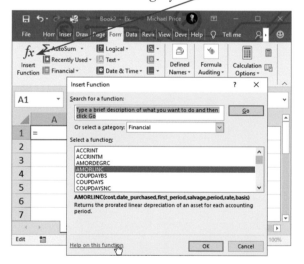

Hot tip

Click **Help on this function** in the **Insert Function** dialog box to get a more detailed description of the function and how to make use of it.

2 Choose a function from the list to see the arguments it requires, plus a brief description

These functions cover all aspects of business financial planning, investment and personal money management. With them you can perform many of the common financial computations, such as the calculation of yield, interest rates, duration, valuation and depreciation.

Payments

The **PMT** function returns the payment amount for a loan based on an interest rate and a constant payment schedule. The syntax for this function is:

PMT(Rate, Number, PV, [FV], [Type])

Rate	The interest rate for the loan.
Number	The number of payments for the loan.
PV	The Present Value or principal of the loan.
FV	The Future Value – loan amount remaining after all payments have been made.
Type	When the payments are due:
	0 – Payments due at end of period (default).
	1 – Payments due at start of period.

Consider a loan of $50,000 over seven years at an annual rate of 5%.

The FV and the Type arguments are optional. If either is omitted, a value of 0 is assumed. The rate must be appropriate to the periods over which payments are made.

1 Calculate the yearly payments required to pay off the loan

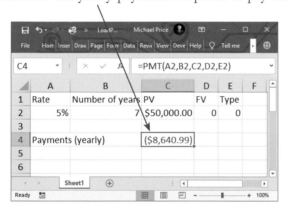

The payment required is shown as a negative number, since it is an outgoing amount.

2 Calculate the quarterly payments required

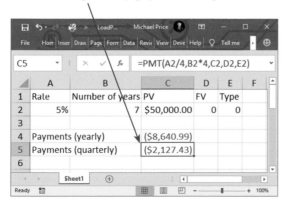

One quarter of the annual rate of interest is used, since payments are to be made quarterly, at the end of each period.

...cont'd

Hot tip

One-twelfth of the annual rate of interest is used, since payments are to be made monthly, at the end of each period.

3 Calculate the monthly payments required

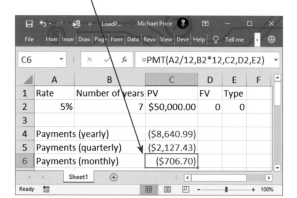

You can calculate the Payment on Principal for any given period, using the **PPMT** function. This has the same arguments as the PMT function, plus the additional argument period. The syntax is:

$$PPMT(Rate, Period, Number, PV, [FV], [Type])$$

Period The period for which Payment on Principal is needed.

Don't forget

Period is a required argument, and is any value between 1 and Number.

1 Calculate the Payment on Principal for the first year, using the example where payments are annual

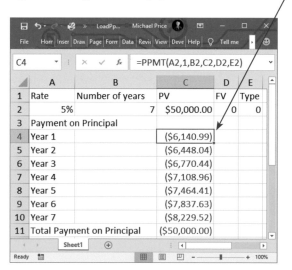

Don't forget

You can see that the total Payments on Principal for all the periods matches the Present Value (the Principal of the loan).

2 Repeat the calculation for each subsequent year, then total all the Payments on Principal

Future Value

If you want to find out the future value of a particular investment that has a constant interest rate and periodic payment, use the **FV** function. The syntax for this function is:

FV (Rate, Number, [Payment], [Lumpsum], [Type])

Rate	Interest rate for the period.
Number	Number of periods.
Payment	Amount saved per period (optional with default of 0).
Lumpsum	The initial investment (optional with default of 0).
Type	Indicates when the payment is required (optional): 0 – Payments due at end of period (default). 1 – Payments due at start of period.

Assume that you make an investment with annual payments of $1,000 where you receive an annual rate of 5%.

1   Calculate the Future Value with payments that are made at the end of each period

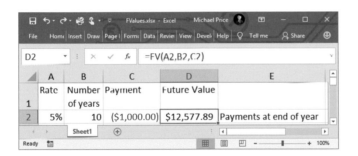

2   Calculate the Future Value when the payments are made at the start of each period

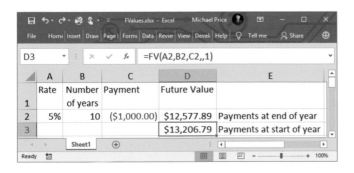

Hot tip

Payment and **Lumpsum** are optional arguments, but you must provide at least one of them.

Hot tip

You must specify the rate adjusted for the period – e.g. 5%/12 for an annual rate of 5% with payments on a monthly basis.

Beware

Since the payments are expenditures, they must be entered into the function as negative numbers.

...cont'd

You can find the Future Value of an initial investment at a given rate of interest.

Suppose you invest a lump sum of $10,000 with the expectation of earning interest of 5% per annum.

1 Calculate the Future Value after 10 years, with the interest being paid annually

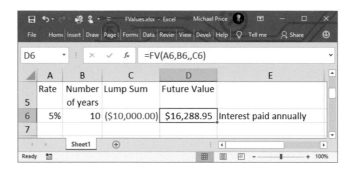

The Payment argument is omitted, and the lump sum is entered as a negative number, since it is an outgoing amount.

2 Repeat the calculation assuming the same lump sum and rate, but with interest applied on a monthly basis, rather than annually

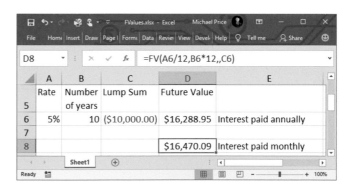

The rate is specified as one-twelfth of the annual interest rate, and the number of periods as 12 times the number of years.

The results for the two calculations illustrate the effect of compounding interest, where interest is applied to the preceding interest payments during the year.

Depreciation

There are several methods of calculating depreciation of an asset. Straight Line Depreciation is the most straightforward method. It depreciates an asset by a fixed amount per period, over the asset's useful life.

The **SLN** function in Excel is based on this method, and it returns the depreciation for a single period. The syntax is:

SLN(Cost, Salvage, Life)

Cost   The initial cost of the asset.
Salvage   The value at the end of the useful life of the asset.
Life   The number of periods in the useful life of the asset.

Assume you have a product purchased at a cost of $25,500, with a useful life of 15 years and a salvage value of $250.

1 Calculate the depreciation for the product for each period

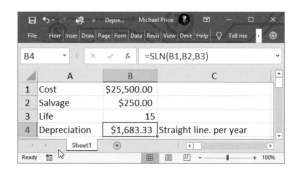

Depreciation is the amount by which the value of an asset reduces in a specific period.

Other depreciation methods ensure accelerated depreciation in the early years of an asset's useful life. For example, Declining Balance Depreciation reduces the value of an asset by a fixed percentage of the asset's value at the start of each period.

The **DB** function in Excel uses this method to return the depreciation during a specified period. The syntax is:

DB(Cost, Salvage, Life, Period, [Month])

This function uses the same arguments as the SLN function, plus:

Period   The period for which you want the depreciation.
Month   The number of months in the first year (optional; default 12).

Period must use the same units as Life. This is normally measured in Years, as implied by the Month argument.

Using the same product details and applying the Declining Balance Depreciation method:

1 Calculate the depreciation for the product in the first year

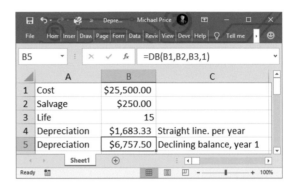

Hot tip

Accelerated depreciation is appropriate for an asset that depreciates more quickly or has greater production capacity in its earlier years. The total amount of depreciation is identical no matter which depreciation method is used.

2 Calculate the depreciation in the final year

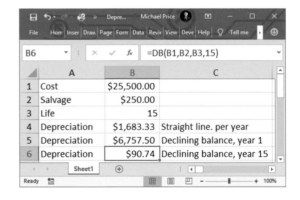

Excel includes three additional functions that involve accelerated depreciation methods.

The **DDB** function returns the depreciation of an asset for the specified period by using the double-declining balance method (or another multiple of declining balance that you specify).

The **VDB** function returns the depreciation of an asset for a specified range of periods, again using the double-declining balance method or another multiple that you specify.

The **SYD** function returns the sum-of-years' digits depreciation of an asset for a specified period, which is another method of calculating accelerated depreciation.

Don't forget

For a product with a useful life of five years, the sum-of-years digits depreciation is 5/15 in the first year and 4/15 in the second year, reducing to 1/15 in the final year.

Statistical Category

Excel provides an extensive range of Statistical functions, which perform calculations from the basic mean, median and mode values to the more complex statistical distribution and probability tests. There is a total of 110 functions, including functions for:

- Averages
- Confidence Intervals
- Count & Frequency
- Deviation & Variance
- Distribution & Tests of Probability
- Finding Largest & Smallest Values
- Percentiles, Quartiles & Rank
- Permutations
- Trend Lines

You can see the full list of functions from the Formulas tab:

1 Select **More Functions** from the **Function Library** group, then select **Statistical**

2 Alternatively, select **Insert Function**, and choose the **Statistical** category

Select a function to review its syntax and a brief description.

3 Select **Help** on this function for a more detailed description

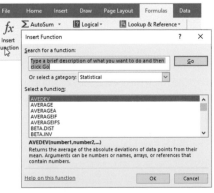

You may be able to derive the same results, using formulas or Math and Trig functions, but the Statistical functions provide consistent and reliable results that are compatible with generally accepted techniques of statistical analysis.

There's also a number of Statistical functions in the Compatibility category. These functions have been replaced by updated and renamed functions, but have been retained to support older worksheets.

Averages

The **AVERAGE** function returns the average (the arithmetic mean) of the arguments specified. The syntax is:

AVERAGE(Number1,[Number2], ...)

Number1	The first or only number, cell reference or range for which you want the average.
Number2	Any additional numbers, cell references or ranges for which you want the average (up to a maximum of 255).

Arguments can either be numbers or names, ranges, or cell references that contain numbers. Cells with text, logical values, or empty cells are ignored, but cells with the value zero will be included in the calculation.

Use the **AVERAGE** function to include logical values and text representations of numbers as part of the calculation.

1 Calculate the average of a set of examination results

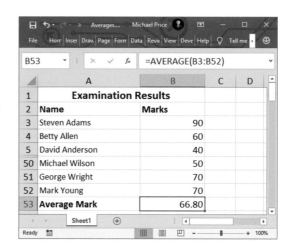

There are Excel functions to calculate the two other types of mean values: the Mode and the Median.

The **MODE.SNGL** function returns the most frequently occurring number in a set of numbers. The **MODE.MULT** function returns an array of the most frequently occurring values in the set.

The **MEDIAN** function will find the middle number of a set of numbers. If there is no single middle value, the mean of the two middle values will be returned.

Sometimes the range of a set of values – the difference between the minimum and the maximum value – is considered as a type of mean value.

...cont'd

2 Display the most frequent mark to be found in the examination results

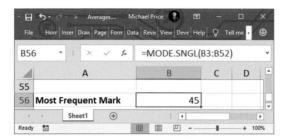

Hot tip

If more than one value occurs the maximum number of times, the first value encountered is displayed.

3 Display the middle mark in the examination results

Don't forget

If there's an even number of values, the mean of the two middle values is displayed. In this example, the two middle values happen to be the same.

There are other averaging functions in Excel.
The **GEOMEAN** function returns the geometric mean (which is the nth root of the product of the n numbers in the set).

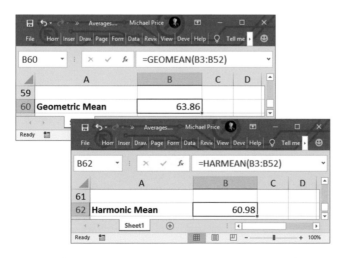

Hot tip

We can illustrate these functions using a set of three numbers – 2, 4, 8:

The Geometric mean is the cube root of 2x4x8, which is 4.

The Harmonic mean is 3 / (1/2+1/4+1/6), which is 3.43.

The **HARMEAN** function returns the harmonic mean (the reciprocal of the average of the reciprocals of all the numbers in the set).

97

Standard Deviation

The standard deviation is a measure of the amount of variation or dispersion of a set of values (known as the population). It is the square root of the variance (the sum of the squares of the differences between the values and their mean). It can be calculated by the **STDEV.P** function. This has the syntax:

STDEV.P(Number1,[Number2], ...)

Number1   The first or only number, cell reference or range.

Number2, ... Any additional numbers, cell references or ranges for a maximum of 255 arguments.

The P in the function name **STDEV.P** stands for Population, which of course refers to all the values in the set.

1   Calculate the standard deviation of the example set of examination results

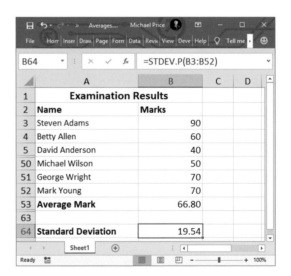

When only a sample of data from the population is available, the **STDEV.S** function should be used. The S in the function name stands for Sample.

A large standard deviation indicates data values may be spread far from the mean, while a small standard deviation shows they are clustered around the mean.

Standard deviation is used to assess the reliability of statistical conclusions – for example, to compare the findings of a poll that is conducted multiple times.

Standard deviation is also used by researchers to distinguish between significant effects and normal random error or variation in measurements, when assessing the results of repeated investigations under varying conditions.

Forecasts

The Forecast functions in Excel allow you to forecast future values based on historical records. If the existing data follows a straight-line progression, you use the **FORECAST.LINEAR** function.

The syntax is:

FORECAST.LINEAR(TargetDate, Values, Dates)

TargetDate   The date for which a forecast is required.

Values   The range of existing values.

Dates   The range of dates for which the values apply.

For example, three years of monthly sales are used to forecast the sales for future months. So, the sales for Jan-21 are forecast based on the sales for Jan-19 to Dec-21.

Hot tip

You must provide the same numbers of values and dates. The dates must be numeric, but can be displayed in any of the date formats.

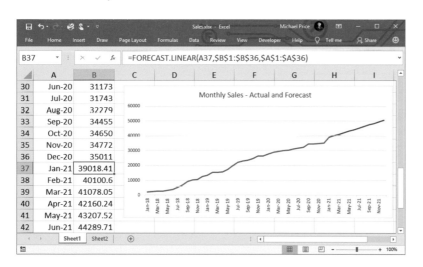

Don't forget

The dates and values are specified using absolute references, while the TargetDate uses a relative reference, making it easy to copy the expression down for further dates.

The graph shows the actual values and the forecast values, which in this example illustrate a linear trend.

If your data is non-linear, you may get more realistic forecasts using the **FORECAST.ETS** function. This uses the Exponential Smoothing (ETS) algorithm.

This function requires the time line to be organized with a constant step between the different points. For example, that could be a monthly time line with values on the 1st of every month, a yearly time line, or a time line of numerical indices.

...cont'd

The syntax of the **FORECAST.ETS** function is:

FORECAST.ETS(TargetDate, Values, Dates,
[Seasonality], [DataCompletion], [Aggregation])

The required arguments are the same as for the **FORECAST. LINEAR** function, but there are some optional arguments to help deal with issues with the structure of the actual data.

In this example the actual data is non-linear, and the forecast algorithm is able to take this into account. The graph illustrates the variable nature of the data, which is replicated in the forecast.

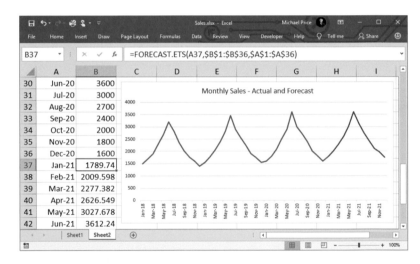

There are several more Forecast functions in Excel:

FORECAST.ETS.CONFINT

Returns a confidence interval for the forecast value at the specified target date.

FORECAST.ETS.SEASONALITY

Returns the length of the repetitive pattern that Excel detects for the specified time series.

FORECAST.ETS.STAT

Returns a statistical value as a result of time series forecasting.

Counting

There are five different **COUNT** functions available in Excel. The **COUNT** function counts cells in the specified set that contain numbers. All other cells are excluded. The syntax is:

COUNT(Value1, [Value2], ...)

The values are cell references or ranges within which you want to count numbers. There can be up to 255 values specified.

1 Count the number of examination results with actual marks specified

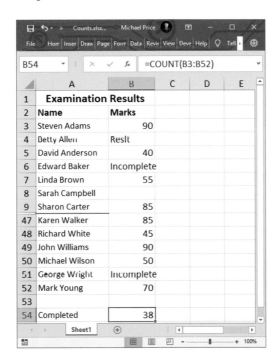

Cells with numbers are counted. Cells with textual comments or cells with no actual entry are not included in the total.

To count cells that have some form of content you'd use the **COUNTA** function. This will count cells with any sort of entry, number, text or logical content, but not blank cells.

To count the blank cells you'd use the **COUNTBLANK** function.

Both functions have the same syntax as the **COUNT** function – one or more cell references or ranges.

Cells with dates and cells with text representations of numbers are counted as numbers by the **COUNT** function. Cells with other text, or logical values or blank (empty) cells are ignored.

The sum of **COUNTA** and **COUNTBLANK** will give the total number of cells in the ranges specified.

...cont'd

2 Calculate the number of examination results that have no mark or comment included

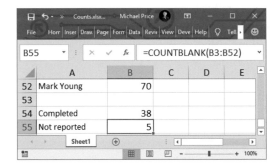

This shows the number of cells in the range that are empty.

To count cells based on a specific value for the content you'd use the **COUNTIF** function. This has the syntax:

=COUNTIF(Range, Condition)

Range The selection of cells to be examined.

Condition The check to be applied to the cell content.

The condition is applied against each cell in the range, and the number of True results is counted.

3 Calculate the number of students scheduled for resits

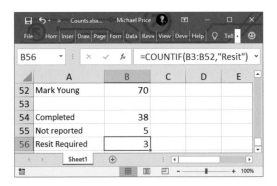

Each cell is checked for the value "Resit" and the total number that is applied against each cell in the range, and the number of True results is counted.

With **COUNTIF** there is one range that is a required argument, but there are no additional optional ranges allowed.

The **COUNTIFS** function allows the checking of multiple ranges, each with an associated criterion. There must be the same number of cells in each range and all the cells at a given level in the ranges must satisfy their respective criterion, to increase the count.

7 Lookup & Reference and Information

Next we look at the Function categories of Lookup & Reference and Information. We review the functions contained in these categories, and examine some of their functions in more detail.

Lookup & Reference Category

Excel comes with a total of 19 Lookup & Reference functions. These functions help you to work with arrays of data, and to cross-reference between different data sets.

There are four groups of functions:

Data Lookup
CHOOSE	Chooses a value from a list of values.
GETPIVOTDATA	Returns data stored in a PivotTable.
HLOOKUP	Returns a value from the indicated row cell.
LOOKUP	Looks up values in a vector or array.
MATCH	Looks up values in a reference or array.
VLOOKUP	Returns a value from indicated column cell.

Area, Column and Row Info
AREAS	Returns the number of areas in reference.
COLUMN	Returns the column number of reference.
COLUMNS	Returns the number of columns in reference.
ROW	Returns the row number of reference.
ROWS	Returns the number of rows in reference.

References to Cell Ranges
ADDRESS	Returns a reference as text to a single cell.
INDEX	Chooses a value from a reference or array.
INDIRECT	Returns a reference indicated by text value.
OFFSET	Returns a reference offset from reference.

Other Functions
FORMULATEXT	Returns a formula at reference as text.
HYPERLINK	Creates a shortcut to external document.
RTD	Retrieves real-time data from a program.
TRANSPOSE	Returns the transpose of an array.

There are several additional functions that are undergoing testing at the time of writing. These include:

FILTER • SORT • SORTBY • UNIQUE
XLOOKUP • XMATCH

When development and testing is completed, these functions will be released to all Excel 2019 and Excel 365 users.

Hot tip

As always, you can select **Formulas**, **Insert Function**, select the category and review the details of each function provided.

Don't forget

Testing is carried out by users who register with Microsoft as Office Insiders and receive early copies of new releases of Office products.

LOOKUP Function

The **LOOKUP** function performs an approximate match lookup and returns a corresponding value. There are two forms of the function: vector and array. The vector form checks in a one-row or one-column range (known as a vector) for a value and returns a value from the same position in a second one-row or one-column range. The syntax is:

LOOKUP(SearchValue, SearchVector, ResultVector)

SearchValue The value that LOOKUP searches for (a number, text, logical value, name or reference).

SearchVector One row or one column range (with text, number or logical values, which are in ascending order).

ResultVector A one-row or column range (this must be the same size as SearchVector).

1 Use LOOKUP to find the grade equivalent to the first student's mark as shown in the Examination Results spreadsheet

Don't forget

The values in the SearchVector range must be in ascending order. The function identifies the location of the largest value in SearchVector that is less than or equal to the SearchValue, and returns the value from the equivalent location in ResultsVector.

105

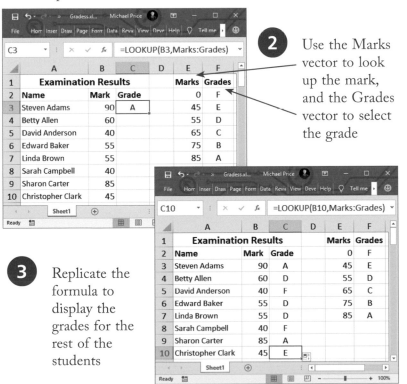

2 Use the Marks vector to look up the mark, and the Grades vector to select the grade

Use absolute references for the vectors, or set up defined names as shown, so you can easily replicate the formula.

3 Replicate the formula to display the grades for the rest of the students

...cont'd

The array form of the **LOOKUP** function is constrained in its operation, and you are recommended to use the alternative **VLOOKUP** and **HLOOKUP** functions.

You can use the array form of LOOKUP to find the grade. This function has the syntax:

LOOKUP(SearchValue, Array)

SearchValue The value that Lookup searches for.

Array The range of cells with search and result values.

If Array has more columns than rows, LOOKUP searches in the first row, and selects from the last row. If it has the same number or more rows than columns, it uses the first and last columns.

4 Use the Array form of LOOKUP to find the grade

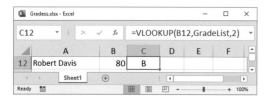

For **VLOOKUP**, the table must have ascending values in column 1.

The VLOOKUP function performs the same operation, but gives you more flexibility. The syntax is:

VLOOKUP(SearchValue, Table, Column, [Approx])

SearchValue The value that VLOOKUP searches for.

Table The range of cells with search and result values (with lookup values in the first column).

Column The column number with the result values.

Approx True for approximate matching (the default). False for exact matching – an optional argument.

5 Use VLOOKUP to find the grade, selecting the result from column 2 and using approximate matching

HLOOKUP has similar arguments to **VLOOKUP**, but searches the first row and selects from the specified row. The table must have ascending values in row 1.

MATCH Function

The **MATCH** function locates the position of a specified value in a row, column, or table. It supports approximate and exact matching, and partial matching using wildcards (* ?).

The syntax of MATCH is:

MATCH(SearchValue,Range,[MatchType])

SearchValue The value to be located.

Range The range of cells to search.

MatchType [optional] Type of match (default is 1):

1	Value less than or equal to SearchValue. (Range must be sorted in ascending order.)
0	Value exactly equal SearchValue. (Range does not need to be sorted.)
-1	Value greater than or equal to SearchValue. (Range must be sorted in descending order.)

Beware

Note that all of the MatchTypes are able to find an exact match for the SearchValue.

1 Use the MATCH function to find the location of Mexico in the Countries table

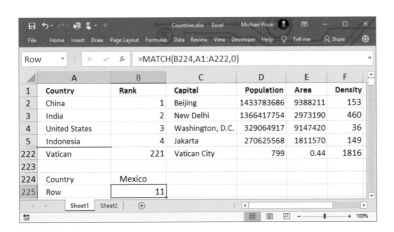

=MATCH(B224,A1:A222,0)

	A	B	C	D	E	F
1	Country	Rank	Capital	Population	Area	Density
2	China	1	Beijing	1433783686	9388211	153
3	India	2	New Delhi	1366417754	2973190	460
4	United States	3	Washington, D.C.	329064917	9147420	36
5	Indonesia	4	Jakarta	270625568	1811570	149
222	Vatican	221	Vatican City	799	0.44	1816
223						
224	Country	Mexico				
225	Row	11				

Hot tip

Since a MatchType of 0 is specified, an exact match is carried out and the range of country names doesn't have to be in sequence.

2 Specify a defined name of row for the cell containing that location value

With the location of Mexico determined, other information about the country can be extracted from the Countries table, using the INDEX function (see pages 108-109).

INDEX Function

The **INDEX** function returns the value at a given position in a range or table. You can use INDEX to retrieve individual values or an entire row or column from the table.

There are two forms of the function: Array and Reference. The syntax of the Array form is:

INDEX(Array,RowNum,[ColNum])

Array   The range of cells.

RowNum   The row position in the array.

ColNum   The column position in the array.

1   Using Row (see page 107), find the capital of Mexico (in column 3 of the Countries table)

Hot tip

If the RowNum (or the ColNum) is set as zero, **INDEX** will return the whole column (or the whole row). For example, to return (and SUM) all the populations, specify row 0 and column 4:

=SUM(INDEX(A2:F222,0,4))

	H	I
	Total Population	
	7703102619	

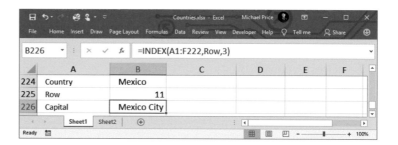

2   Similarly, find Mexico's population (in column 4) and its area (in column 5)

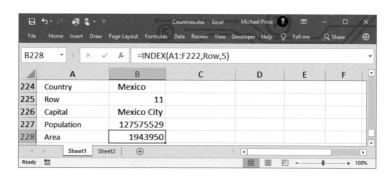

Don't forget

In each case, INDEX uses the row number found by MATCH to locate a specific value in the specified column of the Countries table.

If you suspect that the columns might get rearranged, you can use MATCH to find the one required, rather than providing a specific column number.

3   Find Mexico's population density using MATCH to locate the Density column in the table

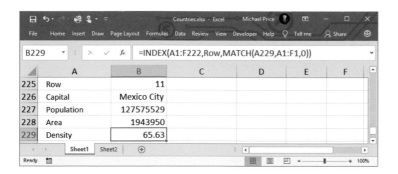

The reference form of INDEX allows you to specify multiple ranges and select which is to be used in the evaluation of INDEX.

The syntax of the reference form is:

INDEX(Reference,RowNum,ColNum,RangeNum)

Reference   The ranges of cells.

RowNum   The row position in the specified range.

ColNum   The column position in the specified range.

RangeNum   The required range from reference.

4   Find the population of Mexico using the reference form of INDEX with several ranges specified

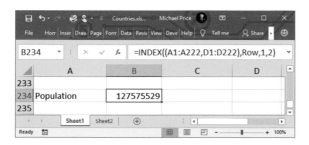

Here reference has two ranges – country names (A1:A222) and population sizes (D1:D222). RangeNum selects the second range and locates the required value in its first (and only) column, using the value of Row to select the entry for Mexico.

Information Category

There are 20 functions within the Information category. These functions provide information about the content, formatting and location of cells in an Excel spreadsheet.

The Information functions fall into four groups, as indicted below:

Error Information

ERROR.TYPE	A number corresponding to an error type.
ISERR	TRUE for any error value except #N/A.
ISERROR	TRUE for any error value.
ISNA	TRUE for the error value #N/A.
NA	The error value #N/A.

Numerical Information

ISEVEN	TRUE if the number is even.
ISNUMBER	TRUE if the value is a number.
ISODD	TRUE if the number is odd.
N	Value converted to a number.

General Information

CELL	Information about the formatting, location, or contents of cell.
INFO	Information about the current operating environment.
SHEET	Sheet number of the referenced sheet.
SHEETS	The number of sheets in a reference.

Data Type

ISBLANK	TRUE if the value is blank.
ISFORMULA	TRUE if there is a reference to a cell that contains a formula.
ISLOGICAL	TRUE if the value is a logical value.
ISNONTEXT	TRUE if the value is not text.
ISREF	TRUE if the value is a reference.
ISTEXT	TRUE if the value is text.
TYPE	A number indicating the data type of a value.

Of these functions, the ISFORMULA, SHEET and SHEETS functions were first introduced in Excel 2013 and so are not available in previous versions of Excel.

ERROR.TYPE Function

The **ERROR.TYPE** function returns a number corresponding to one of the Excel error values, or returns a #N/A error if no error exists. You might use ERROR.TYPE in an IF or IFS function to test for an error value and return an appropriate text string as a message, instead of the error value.

The syntax is simply:

ERROR.TYPE(ErrorValue)

ErrorValue The error value whose identifying number you want to find.

ErrorValue	Number returned
#NULL!	1
#DIV/0!	2
#VALUE!	3
#REF!	4
#NAME?	5
#NUM!	6
#N/A	7
#GETTING_DATA	8
Anything else	#N/A

1 Calculate the unit price given the amount and the quantity

With the initial values set to zero, the formula gives a #DIV0! result.

2 Replicate the calculation with some realistic values

The formula now gives a numeric result rather than an error.

You can use ERROR.TYPE to investigate the results of the calculation, and perhaps provide a more meaningful message to the worksheet user.

Although ErrorValue can be the actual error value, it will usually be a reference to a cell containing a formula whose results you want to check.

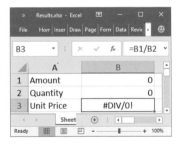

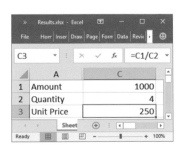

If cells are initially empty, they will be treated as having zero values, and this may imply errors in formulas until the actual data has been entered.

Hot tip

A cell may display #### when the column is too narrow or with a negative number in a Date field. ERROR.TYPE does not see this as an error, and so will return a #N/A response.

| Date | ######## |
| Error.type | #N/A |

Beware

You should check whether a numeric result has been returned, perhaps using the ISNUMBER function, before you check for the Divide by Zero error.

...cont'd

3 Use ERROR.TYPE to check the form of the results

The initial result is identified as error number 2, the Divide by Zero error.

The subsequent result is not an error, so the response is #N/A, meaning that no value is available since no error has been found.

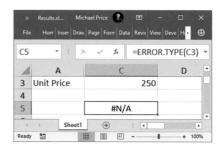

When there is an error detected, you can use the results from ERROR.TYPE to provide a more meaningful message.

4 Use the IFS function along with the ERROR.TYPE function to provide a message "Quantity is Zero" when the Divide by Zero error message is detected

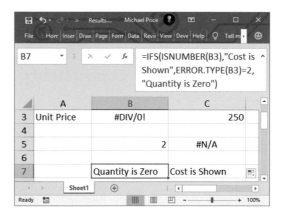

The ERROR.TYPE check is found to be True, so the IFS function displays the message provided.

The alternative message "Cost is Shown" is displayed for the subsequent calculation, which returns a numeric result, as detected by the ISNUMBER function.

IS Functions

There are twelve **IS** functions in the Information category. They include: ISBLANK • ISERR • ISERROR • ISEVEN ISFORMULA • ISLOGICAL • ISNA • ISNONTEXT ISNUMBER • ISODD • ISREF • ISTEXT
Each function carries out a check and returns TRUE or FALSE as the result. The syntax for all the IS functions is the same. Eg.:

> ISBLANK(Value)

Value   An empty cell, error, logical value, text, number, or reference, or a name referring to any of these.

Some of the functions deal with the actual content of the referenced cell while others deal with the result produced by a formula in the cell. Looking at the two Unit Price calculations, ISFORMULA confirms that both calculations are formula.

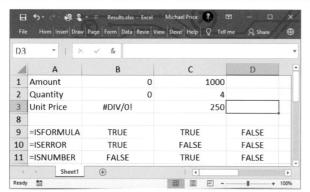

ISERROR checks the results of the calculations, and finds the first as an error while the second is not. ISNUMBER also checks the results and finds the second is a number, but the first is not.

You can use an IF function in combination with an IS function to generate plain text messages describing the current situation.

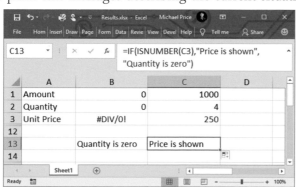

INFO Function

The **INFO** function returns information about the current environment, including platform, Excel version, number of worksheets in a workbook, etc.

The syntax of the INFO function is:

=INFO(InfoType)

InfoType   The information type to be retrieved (entered in double quotation marks).

There are seven types of information available:

"directory"	Path of the current directory or folder.
"numfile"	Number of active worksheets in open workbooks.
"origin"	First visible cell at upper left.
"osversion"	Operating system version.
"recalc"	Recalculation mode.
"release"	Excel version.
System	Operating system name.

Here are examples of the information retrieved, for a system in a Windows environment where Excel is loaded, and there are two separate workbooks open, each with one active worksheet.

Beware

The InfoType value can be in lowercase, uppercase or mixed case. The value will always be recognized, as long as it is spelled correctly.

Hot tip

114

In previous versions of Excel, entries "memavail", "memused", and "totmem" returned memory information. These information types are no longer supported and if used now would return a #N/A error.

=INFO("memused")	#N/A
=INFO("memavail")	#N/A
=INFO("totmem")	#N/A
=INFO("memory")	#VALUE!
=INFO("othertext")	#VALUE!

Any other text entry will give a #VALUE! error.

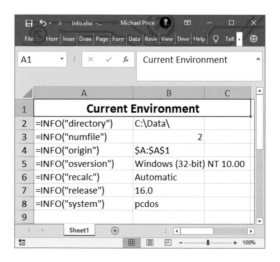

CELL Function

The **CELL** function returns information about the formatting, location, or contents of a cell. The syntax of the CELL function is:

CELL(InfoType,Reference)

InfoType   Text value specifying the cell information needed.
Reference   The cell location (optional).

InfoType	Information Returned
"address"	Reference to the cell, as text.
"col"	Column number of the cell.
"color"	The value 1 if the cell is formatted in color for negative values; otherwise 0.
"contents"	Value of the cell (not the formula).
"filename"	Full filename that contains the cell, as text.
"format"	Text value corresponding to the number format of the cell (see example below).
"prefix"	Single quote (') for left-aligned text. Double quote mark (") for right-aligned text. Caret (^) for centered text. Backslash (\) for fill-aligned text. Empty text ("") for anything else.
"protect"	The value 1 if the cell is locked; else 0.
"row"	Row number of the cell.
"type"	"b" for an empty cell. "l" for a text constant. "v" for anything else.
"width"	The column width of the cell, rounded to integer, plus a Logical value: True if it is the default width or False if the width was set by the user.

If Reference is a range of cells, the upper left cell of the range is used. If there is no reference, the last cell to have been changed is taken.

The CELL function returns empty text ("") as the filename if the worksheet has not yet been saved.

Each unit of column width is equal to the width of one character in the default font size.

1 Show the same number displayed with various formats

If you then apply a different format to a cell, you must recalculate the worksheet (press **F9**) to update the results of the CELL function.

| | CellForma... | Michael Price | | — □ × |
| File | Hom | Inser | Draw | Page | Forn | Data | Revie | View | Deve | Help | |

C5   fx   =CELL("FORMAT",A5)

	A	B	C
1	15.6		G
2	15.60		F2
3	1/15/00 2:24 PM		D2
4	1/15/00 14:24		D4
5	14:24:00		D8
6	1.56E+01		S2
7	15 3/5		G
8			

Sheet1   ⊕

Ready   100%

TYPE Function

The empty cell is flagged as "b", the text cell is "l", while the number, logical and error cells are all "v".

The CELL function with the "type" InfoType identifies a cell as empty, or containing a text constant, or as anything else.

Here are examples of cell types being identified:

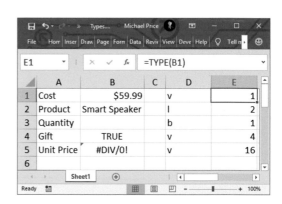

A somewhat different analysis is carried out by the TYPE function. This function has the syntax:

$$TYPE(Value)$$

Value	Reference to any Excel value, or the value itself.

Value	Result
Number	1
Text	2
Logical value	4
Error value	16
Array	64

With the **TYPE** function, logical and error values are now distinguished. However, empty cells are treated as numbers (the value 0 being assumed).

For the example cells used above, the TYPE function returns these results:

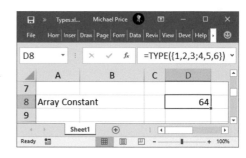

The TYPE function is also able to recognize array values. Applied to an array constant, the TYPE function provides this result:

8 Database and Engineering

The Database category includes functions that perform operations on data that is in an organized table structure, while the Engineering category carries out calculations such as Bessel functions, complex numbers and conversions.

Database Category

The Database category incorporates 12 Database functions with which you can calculate statistics such as total, average, minimum, maximum and count, in a specified field of the data list and for records that match the criteria provided.

The functions included are:

DAVERAGE	Returns the average of selected database entries.
COUNT	Counts cells that contain numbers in a database.
DCOUNTA	Counts nonblank cells in a database.
DGET	Extracts a single record matching specified criteria.
DMAX	Selects maximum from selected database entries.
DMIN	Selects minimum from selected database entries.
DPRODUCT	Multiplies values in a specified field of the records in the database that match the specified criteria.
DSTDEV	Estimates standard deviation based on a sample of selected database entries.
DSTDEVP	Calculates the standard deviation based on the entire population of selected database entries.
DSUM	Adds numbers in the field column of records in the database that match the specified criteria.
DVAR	Estimates variance based on a sample from selected database entries.
DVARP	Calculates variance based on the entire population of selected database entries.

All Excel Database functions use the same syntax – for example:

DAVERAGE(Database,Field,Criteria)

Database	The range of cells containing the data, with labels for each column in the top row.
Field	The column that is to be used in calculations: – A reference to the column name, or – The column name inside quotation marks, or – The column number in the data range.
Criteria	The range of cells that contain the conditions that determine which records are to be included in the calculations, with the label of the column(s) to be filtered and the condition(s) to be satisfied provided under the label.

Excel Database

The Database functions work with lists or tables of data, arranged so that the first row provides field names while the subsequent rows each provide one set of related field values (one record).

Here is an example list with each row related to an individual country, providing details such as country name, capital city, population, area, dialing code and region.

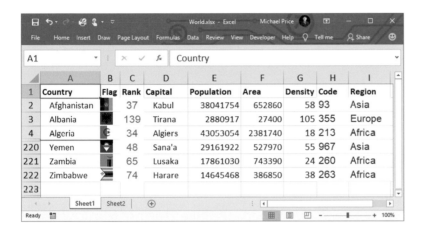

The Database functions treat the names and records as an Excel database, so you should define a name for the whole range.

1 Select all the cells in the database – labels and records

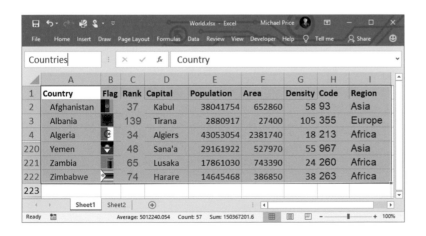

2 Click in the Name box, type the name Countries and press **Enter** to define the name for the range

Hot tip

In the example, the records are sequenced by country name. However, they could be in any sequence or even randomly ordered.

Don't forget

The rows below the list should be empty. This will make it easier to add or insert additional records into the database.

Don't forget

Rows 5-219 are hidden, to make it easier to see the database, but they are still included in the named selection.

...cont'd

You can check in the Name Manager to see the new defined name that you have created.

1 Select Formulas and click the Name Manager entry in the Defined Names group

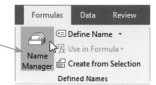

The Name Manager list will be displayed, and you can review the characteristics associated with the countries.

You can use this name with any of the Database functions. For example, to find the average population in the region of Asia:

1 In an area of the worksheet alongside the data list, type the heading **Region** and below this the value **Asia**

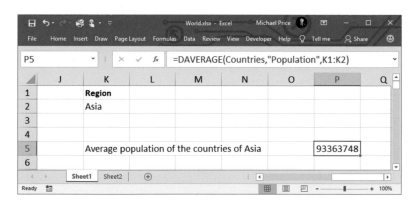

2 To calculate the average, enter the formula
=DAVERAGE(Countries,"Population",K1:K2)

All the countries in the Asia region are selected and their populations will be summed and averaged.

DGET Function

The **DGET** function gets a single value in the requested field from the record in the specified database that matches the criteria provided. To use DGET to display the capital city of Mexico:

1 Specify a criteria range with **Country** as the heading and **Mexico** as the value and enter the formula
=DGET(Countries,"Capital",L1:L2)

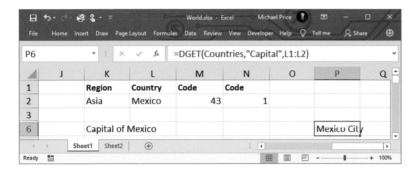

The Mexico record is located and its capital is extracted.

You can use a number as the criteria value.

1 Request the country with dialing code 43, using the formula **=DGET(Countries,"Country",M1:M2)** and the country of Austria is identified

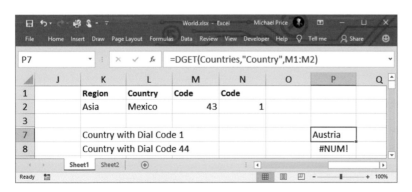

2 Similarly, identify the country that has a dialing code of 1 using **=DGET(Countries,"Country",N1:N2)**

The response #NUM! is returned, indicating that DGET has found more than one record that satisfies the criteria.

121

Hot tip

You don't need to enter the full name. Enter the first few characters (for example, Mex) and DGET will identify the record that contains the value beginning with those letters.

Hot tip

If there is no record that matches the criteria, then DGET will give #VALUE! as an error response.

DSUM Function

The **DSUM** function returns the sum of values from a specified field in the records of the database that match the criteria.

The DSUM function selects all the records with a region of Asia, and sums all their Population fields.

1 Calculate the total population for the region of Asia

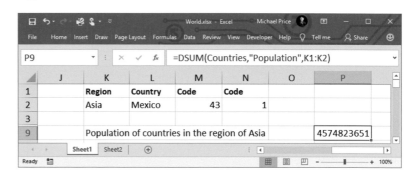

If a partial criteria value is provided, DSUM selects all records where the value begins with the criteria supplied.

2 Calculate the total population of the region of Eur...

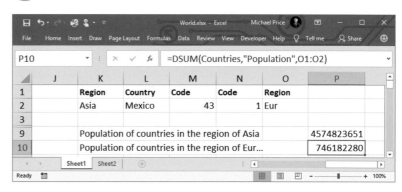

If the criteria value provided is blank, all records will be selected.

The DSUM function can make use of wildcards with the criteria values:
* zero or more chars
? any one character
~ for literal character
(for example, ~? for a literal question mark).

3 Calculate the population of all the countries in the list

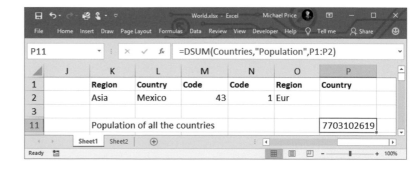

122

Excel Tables

The Database functions also work with Excel tables. Again, the data structure must contain a header row followed by data rows.

To create a table from such a list:

1 Select the whole data range – header row plus data rows

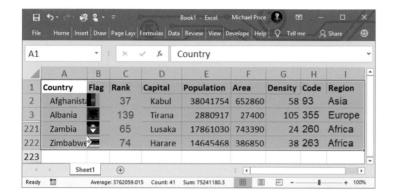

This is the same data used previously to show the Database functions with Excel data lists.

2 Select the **Insert** tab, then click the **Table** button in the **Tables** group

3 Check the full data range is specified and make sure **My table has headers** is selected, then click **OK**

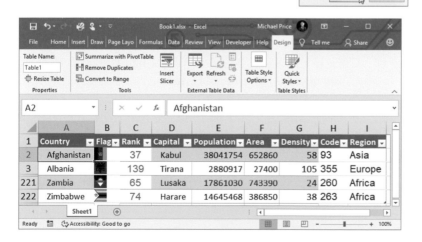

Click in the table and select the **Design** tab and you'll see that a default name such as Table1 has been assigned.

The table is generated with the default banding style. A Filter button is added alongside the header in each column.

...cont'd

Open the Name Manager (see page 16) and you will see that the table name refers to all the data rows but excludes the header row. It is therefore unsuitable for the Database functions.

Hot tip

In Database functions the Database range should incorporate the whole list – labels and data records.

To define a name that refers to the whole table:

1 Select the complete table – the header row plus all of the data rows

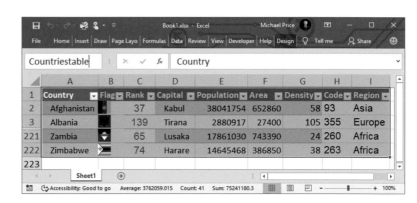

Don't forget

If you have added a Totals row to your table, this should be excluded from the selection for the purpose of Database functions.

2 Click in the Name box then type a name (e.g. Countriestable) and press **Enter**

Open the Name Manager and you will see that the name refers to =Table1[#All], which includes the headers and the data.

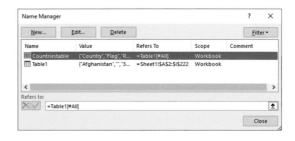

Table Used By Database

You can perform any of the Database functions, using this name as the database. For example:

1 Get the population density of China

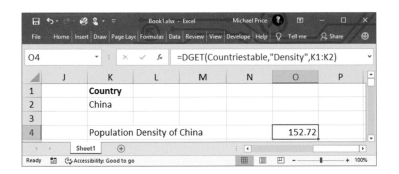

The criteria are used to identify the data row for China in the data range, and the density is extracted.

2 Find the maximum population density for a country

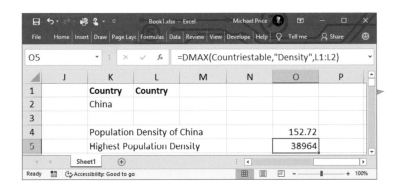

The empty cell in the criteria means that the DMAX function searches the records for all the countries to find the maximum density.

3 Get the country that has that maximum density

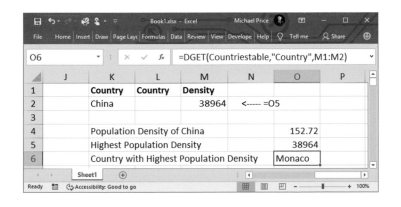

The value for the criteria range is set to equal the result from the previous formula, which is the maximum density, then the country with that density is located.

Engineering Category

There are 54 functions in the Engineering category. These functions perform the most commonly used engineering calculations, including those relating to converting between different units of measurement, or bases, Bessel functions and complex numbers.

The Engineering functions may be divided into the following subcategories:

Converting Between Units of Measurement
CONVERT

Bessel Functions
BESSELI • BESSELJ • BESSEL • BESSELY

Converting Between Bases
BIN2DEC • BIN2HEX • BIN2OCT • DEC2BIN
DEC2HEX • DEC2OCT • HEX2BIN • HEX2DEC
HEX2OCT • OCT2BIN • OCT2DEC • OCT2HEX

The Error Function
ERF • ERF.PRECISE • ERFC • ERFC.PRECISE

Bitwise Functions
BITAND • BITOR • BITXOR • BITLSHIFT • BITRSHIFT

Testing Numeric Values
DELTA • GESTEP

Complex Numbers
COMPLEX • IMABS • IMAGINARY • IMARGUMENT
IMCONJUGATE • IMCOS • IMCOSH • IMCOT
IMCSC • IMCSCH • IMDIV • IMEXP • IMLN
IMLOG10 • IMLOG2 • IMPOWER • IMPRODUCT
IMREAL • IMSEC • IMSECH • IMSIN • IMSINH,
IMSQRT • IMSUB • IMSUM • IMTAN

Some of these functions were added to newer versions of Excel and so are not available in earlier versions. For example, the ERF.PRECISE and ERFC.PRECISE functions were added to Excel 2010, while the BITAND, BITOR, BITXOR, BITLSHIFT, IMCOSH, IMCOT, IMCSC, IMCSCH, IMSEC, IMSECH, IMSINH and IMTAN functions were added to Excel 2013.

Engineers may also use the functions in the Math & Trig and the Statistical categories, and the Analysis ToolPak add-in (see page 151).

Some of the functions are also generally used in other disciplines as well as engineering, in particular those related to conversions.

CONVERT Function

The **CONVERT** function changes a number from one measurement system to another. For example, CONVERT can change a weight in pounds to a weight in grams. The syntax is:

CONVERT(Number,FromUnit,ToUnit)

Number   The value in FromUnit that is to be converted.

FromUnit   The original unit for Number (a text string).

ToUnit   The target unit for Number (a text string).

CONVERT handles the following measurement systems:

- Weight and Mass
- Time
- Force
- Magnetism
- Volume
- Information
- Distance
- Pressure
- Power
- Temperature
- Area
- Speed

For each measurement system, a comprehensive set of units is supported. For example, the following units are recognized as weight and mass measurements:

Unit	Description
g	Gram
sg	Slug
lbm	Pound mass (avoirdupois)
u	U (atomic mass unit)
ozm	Ounce mass (avoirdupois)
grain	Grain
cwt	U.S. (short) hundredweight
shweight	U.S. (short) hundredweight
uk_cwt	Imperial hundredweight
lcwt	Imperial hundredweight
hweight	Imperial hundredweight
stone	Stone
ton	Ton
uk_ton	Imperial ton
LTON	Imperial ton
brton	Imperial ton

The units are case-sensitive, so "lton" would not be recognized as an Imperial ton (the correct unit being "LTON").

Hot tip

If the data types of the arguments are incorrect, CONVERT returns a #VALUE! error.

127

Don't forget

If the unit type specified is not recognized, or if the From and To units are in different measurement systems, CONVERT returns a #N/A error.

...cont'd

Instead of 1,000 "g" you can specify 1 "kg", using the Kilo prefix, thus defining the Kilogram unit.

The price history table from **Yahoo! Finance** provides information in reverse date sequence, on a daily, weekly, or monthly basis. Use the **Adjusted Close** values to ensure that the prices are comparable over time.

1 Convert 77° Fahrenheit to Centigrade (result is 25°)

2 Convert 1,000 grams to pounds (result is 2.20)

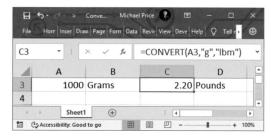

3 Convert 60 miles to kilometers (result is 96.56)

4 Convert 10 feet to seconds (result is a #N/A error)

The From unit and the To unit are from different measurement systems, so this is an invalid conversion.

The error is that two different measurement systems have been used.

Convert Between Bases

There 12 functions providing conversion between pairs of the Binary, Decimal, Hexadecimal and Octal bases. For example:

1 Convert 64 Decimal to Octal (result is 100)

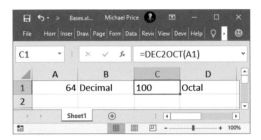

2 Convert 7C Hexadecimal to Decimal (result is 124)

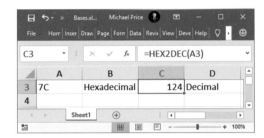

3 Convert 1010101 Binary to Octal 4 places (result is 0125)

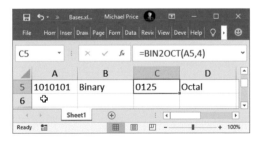

4 Convert 20 Octal to Hexadecimal (result is 10)

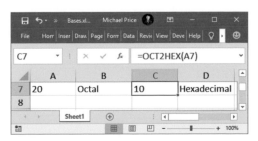

DELTA Function

The **DELTA** function tests whether a supplied number is equal to a second supplied number (if provided) or to zero. The syntax is:

DELTA(Value1,Value2)

Value1 This is the value to be checked.

Value2 This is the value to check against.

If Value2 is not provided, a value of zero is assumed.

Hot tip

The Kronecker Delta (named after Leopold Kronecker) is a function of two variables that has the value 1 if the variables are equal, and 0 otherwise.

Hot tip

The results of formulas =4+4 and =2^3 are compared, and a result of 1 indicates that they give the same value.

Hot tip

Two values displayed with no decimal places both show as 2, but the Delta function indicates that they are not actually equal.

1 Confirm that the results of two formulas are the same

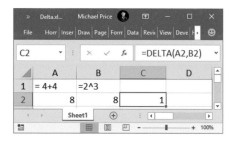

2 Confirm that two apparently identical numbers are actually different values

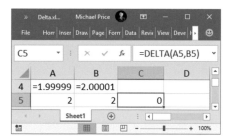

3 Compare a value with the default value, to confirm that the value does not equal zero

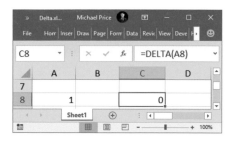

GESTEP Function

GESTEP, the second function for testing numeric values, checks how a number compares to a supplied threshold value. It returns the value 1 (True) when the number is greater than or equal to the step size. It returns the value 0 (False) when the number is less than the step size.

The syntax of the function is:

GESTEP(Number,[Step])

Number   The number to be tested.

Step   The step size that Number is to be compared to.

To illustrate the use of the GESTEP function:

1   Check that the number in A1 is greater than or equal to the step value in B1

The value 1 is returned, indicating it is True that the number is greater than or equal to the step value.

2   Check that the number in A3 is not greater than or equal to the step value in B3

The value 0 is returned, indicating False – the number is not greater than or equal to the step value.

The function will also check against a default value of 0 (zero).

The Step argument is optional. If it is omitted, the default value 0 (zero) will be used for the comparison.

131

The number and step can be literal values, numeric text strings or expressions that return a value. If the argument does not resolve to a number, a #VALUE! error is displayed.

Check that the number in A5 is greater than or equal to the value 0 (zero)

Since no Step value is provided, Number is compared to the default value 0 (zero), and is found to be greater than or equal.

You can use the IF function to test the result of a GESTEP formula, and the TRUE function to return an explicit True or False.

For example, A7 is greater than or equal to B7, so the GESTEP function returns the value 1, which is detected by the IF function, so the associated TRUE function returns an explicit True value.

However, A9 is less than B9, so the GESTEP function returns the value 0, which is detected by the IF function, which returns a default response, an explicit False value.

You could also use the IF function to return alternative text values – for example, =IF(GESTEP(A9,B9),"Pass","Fail").

Beware

When the first argument of the IF function is the value 1 or the logical True value, it displays the logical False value (or the value of the third argument if provided). See page 67 for more details of this function.

Hot tip

The TRUE function takes no arguments and can be entered as TRUE() or just simply TRUE as in the examples.

9

Compatibility, Cube and Web

The Compatibility category includes functions that have been replaced by newer, improved functions, but are included in Excel to provide backward compatibility for spreadsheets created in older versions of Excel. The final two categories, Cube and Web, are for use with external data content.

You may have created workbooks in older versions of Excel that use functions replaced or updated in newer versions of Excel. The functions in the Compatibility category ensure that these workbooks will continue to operate in the newer versions of Excel.

Compatibility Category

In Excel 2010 and later versions, certain functions were replaced with new functions that provided improved accuracy, with names that better reflected their usage. The original functions were retained in the Compatibility category and can still be used – for example, in spreadsheets that were created for an earlier version of Excel. However, if backward compatibility isn't required, you should use the new functions instead.

If you're using Excel 2007, you'll find the older functions in the Statistical or Math & Trig categories.

There are 42 functions in the Compatibility category, including the following:

BETADIST	BETAINV	BINOMDIST
CEILING	CHIDIST	CHIINV
CHITEST	CONCATENATE	CONFIDENCE
COVAR	CRITBINOM	EXPONDIST
FDIST	FINV	FLOOR
FORECAST	FTEST	GAMMADIST
GAMMAINV	HYPGEOMDIST	LOGINV
LOGNORMDIST	MODE	NEGBINOMDIST
NORMDIST	NORMINV	NORMSDIST
NORMSINV	PERCENTILE	PERCENTRANK
POISSON	QUARTILE	RANK
STDEV	STDEVP	TDIST
TINV	TTEST	VAR
VARP	WEIBULL	ZTEST

To replace these functions and to add capabilities, new functions were added to the versions of Excel that came after Excel 2007.

Excel 2010 included 61 additional functions:

AGGREGATE	BETA.DIST	BETA.INV
BINOM.DIST	BINOM.INV	CEILING.PRECISE
CHISQ.DIST	CHISQ.DIST.RT	CHISQ.INV
CHISQ.INV.RT	CHISQ.TEST	CONFIDENCE.NORM
CONFIDENCE.T	COVARIANCE.P	COVARIANCE.S
ERF.PRECISE	ERFC.PRECISE	EXPON.DIST
F.DIST	F.DIST.RT	F.INV
F.INV.RT	F.TEST	FLOOR.PRECISE
GAMMA.DIST	GAMMA.INV	GAMMALN.PRECISE
HYPGEOM.DIST	ISO.CEILING	LOGNORM.DIST
LOGNORM.INV	MODE.MULT	MODE.SNGL
NEGBINOM.DIST	NETWORKDAYS.INT	NORM.DIST
NORM.INV	NORM.S.DIST	NORM.S.INV

The additional functions in Excel 2010 included 39 renamed functions and 22 new functions.

PERCENTILE.EXC   PERCENTILE.INC   PERCENTRANK.EXC
PERCENTRANK.INC   POISSON.DIST   QUARTILE.EXC
QUARTILE.INC   RANK.AVG   RANK.EQ
STDEV.P   STDEV.S   T.DIST
T.DIST.2T   T.DIST.RT   T.INV
T.INV.2T   T.TEST   VAR.P
VAR.S   WEIBULL.DIST   WORKDAY.INTL
Z.TEST

Excel 2013 included 51 new functions:

ACOT   ACOTH   ARABIC
BASE   BINOM.DIST.RANGE   BITAND
BITLSHIFT   BITOR   BITRSHIFT
BITXOR   CEILING.MATH   COMBINA
COT   COTH   CSC
CSCH   DAYS   DECIMAL
ENCODEURL   FILTERXML   FLOOR.MATH
FORMULATEXT   GAMMA   GAUSS
IFNA   IMCOSH   IMCOT
IMCSC   IMCSCH   IMSEC
IMSECH   IMSINH   IMTAN
ISFORMULA   ISO.CEILING   ISOWEEKNUM
MUNIT   NUMBERVALUE   PDURATION
PERMUTATIONA   PHI   RRI
SEC   SECH   SHEET
SHEETS   SKEW.P   UNICHAR
UNICODE   WEBSERVICE   XOR

Excel 2016 included 5 new functions:

FORECAST.ETS   FORECAST.ETS.CONFINT
FORECAST.ETS.SEASONALITY   FORECAST.ETS.STAT
FORECAST.LINEAR

Excel 2019 and Excel 365 included 6 new functions:

CONCAT   IFS   MAXIFS
MINIFS   SWITCH   TEXTJOIN

A number of functions received algorithm changes in Excel 2010 to improve accuracy and performance.

The new functions are incompatible with earlier versions of Excel, but you can use the Compatibility Checker (see page 143) to help make the necessary changes to your worksheets.

CONCATENATE Function

The Excel CONCATENATE function has been relegated to the Compatibility category, but it will still function. It is designed to concatenate or join up to 30 text items and return the result as a single text string.

The syntax of the CONCATENATE function is:

CONCATENATE(Text1,Text2,[Text3]...)

Text1   The first text item to join together.

Text2   The second text item to join together.

Text3   The third text item to join together.

There must be at least two, and a maximum of 30 text items. Each can be a text, a number or a reference to a single cell containing a text string or a number (which gets converted to text).

The CONCAT function (see page 81) replaces CONCATENATE in Excel 2019 and Excel 365. This function supports up to 255 text items, to a maximum of 8,192 characters.

1   Concatenate the headings for columns A, B and C

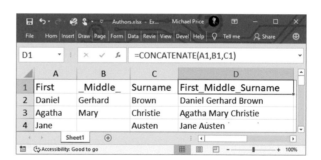

If you want something between the text items you must include a suitable text value enclosed in double quotes, such as "_" or " ", with each such value being one of the 30 arguments.

The specified text items are joined, with no characters or spaces between them, to form a single text string.

2   Concatenate text strings with a space between each

The Ampersand operator & is an alternative to the CONCATENATE function, giving the same result in a shorter and perhaps more readable formula.

 3 Combine text items, with a space between each, using the Ampersand character

The Ampersand text concatenation operator is available in all versions of Excel.

The text items specified are joined, with a space inserted between each of them.

The TEXTJOIN function (see page 82) added in Excel 2019 and Excel 365 allows you to join text items using a specified separator string. The text items can include text strings and ranges of cells containing text strings, and there can be up to 252 such text arguments. There is also an option to skip over any empty cells in the text arguments provided.

4 Combine text items, with a space between each, skipping any empty cells

The TEXTJOIN function can return a text string up to 32,767 characters in length. If the result exceeds this, a #VALUE! error is generated.

The text items in the specified range are joined, with a space between each. There is an empty cell in the range in this example, so that cell is skipped.

FORECAST Function

This calculates, or predicts, a future value by using existing values. The predicted value is a Y value for a given X value. The known values are existing X values and Y values, and the new value is predicted by using linear regression. You can use this function, for example, to predict future sales, inventory requirements, or consumer trends.

The syntax of the FORECAST function is:

FORECAST(X, Yvalues, Xvalues)

There are three arguments, all of which are required:

X	The data point at which to predict a Y value.
Yvalues	The dependent array or range of data.
Xvalues	The independent array or range of data.

To illustrate the use of FORECAST we will use the range of attendance numbers for the US Open tennis tournament, shown in sequence for the years 2013 to 2019.

1 Forecast the attendance numbers for the year 2020, based on the actual numbers for 2013 to 2019

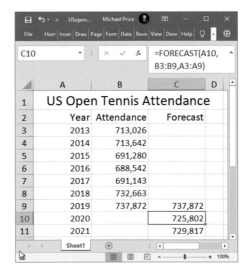

2 Similarly, forecast the attendance value for 2021

There must be the same number of entries in the Xvalues and Yvalues ranges, and the X value must be numeric.

The Forecast function uses linear regression to calculate the value of Y associated with the specified value of X.

Use absolute references in the ranges (e.g. B9) if you want to copy the formula down to make additional forecasts.

You can use the 2D Line Chart to illustrate how the historical and forecast attendance numbers relate.

3 Select all the data and the headings, then from the **Insert** tab select **Insert Line** or **Area Chart**

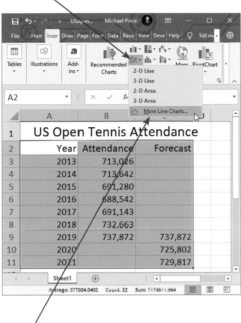

The Insert Line or Area Chart option is in the Charts group on the Insert tab.

4 Select **More Line Charts...**, and choose the **Line** chart plotting attendance and forecast by years

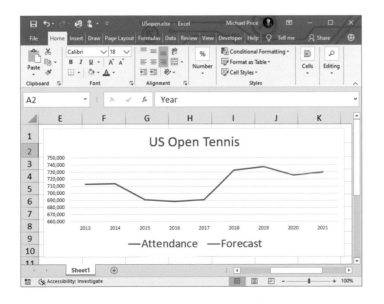

Insert, Recommended Charts will suggest the types of chart that may be appropriate for the data you have selected.

RANK Function

The RANK function returns the rank or order of a numeric value in a list of values. The list does not have to be sorted, but RANK gives the position the value would have if the list was to be sorted. The value can be ranked descending or ascending.

The syntax of the RANK function is:

RANK(Number,List,[Order])

Number	The value whose rank you want to find.
List	Reference to the range of values to rank against.
Order	A value to specify how to rank: 0 (or omitted argument) means rank descending. 1 (or any non-zero value) means rank ascending.

Take the scores and absences for a group of students.

1 Rank the Score values, using descending order

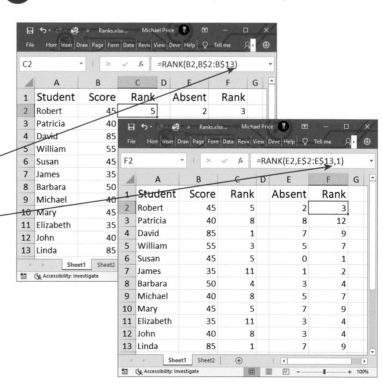

2 Rank the Absent values, using ascending order

If Number matches several values in List, the top rank of that group of values will be returned.

There's no order value with the Score Rank, so values are ranked descending. With the Absent Rank, there's an order value of 1 specified, so values are ranked ascending.

...cont'd

In Excel 2010 and later, the RANK function was replaced by the RANK.EQ function, with the same syntax, arguments and results.

The RANK.AVG function was also added. This shares the same syntax and arguments, but when it detects multiple matches for Number, it returns the average rank of that group of values.

1 Use the RANK.AVG function to rank the Score values, based on descending order

The results for RANK.EQ are exactly the same as those for RANK. You are advised to use the newer RANK.EQ, in case the older function is removed from a future version of Excel.

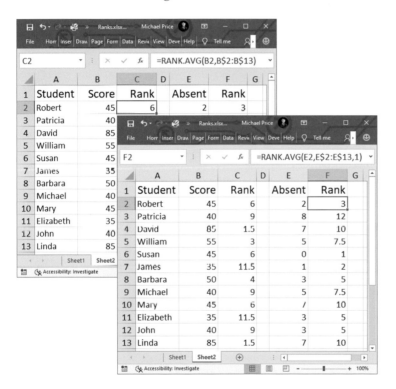

In each case, the vertical references for the List range are specified with absolute addresses (for example, $B2:$B13), making it possible to copy the formula down for other values.

2 Use the RANK.AVG function to rank the Absent values, based on ascending order

The ranks for values that have duplicate matches are averaged. For example, the score of 45 is shared by three students and the value 45 is positions 7, 6 and 5 in the sorted list, so the assigned rank is the average value 6.

Similarly, two students are absent 5 times, with 5 being 7 and 8 in the sorted list, so the assigned rank is the average value 7.5.

Compatibility Mode

1 In your current copy of Excel, open an .xlxs workbook

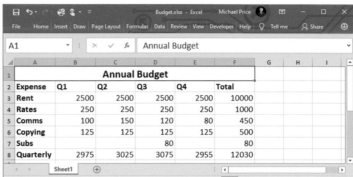

Hot tip

You are switched into compatibility mode to ensure your worksheet can be used in an older version of Excel.

2 Select **File**, **Save As** and choose the file location

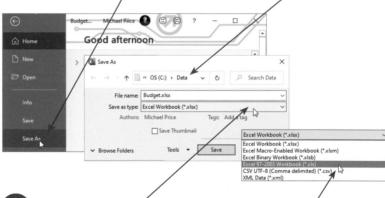

3 Click on the **Save as type** box and select to save the workbook as an Excel 97-2003 Workbook (*.xls) file

Hot tip

When you open the .xls workbook using your current Excel, you'll see that Compatibility Mode is specified alongside the workbook name.

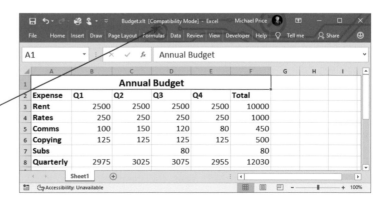

Compatibility Checker

1 Open the .xls file in the current version of Excel, and add a function new in that version – for example, TEXTJOIN

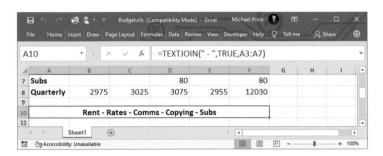

Click **Find** to locate the formula with the unavailable function, and click **Help** for more information about compatibility issues in Excel.

2 Select **File**, **Save** and the Compatibility Checker warns you that the workbook refers to a function that is not available in earlier versions of Excel

3 Select **Continue** to save the workbook anyway

4 Open the .xls workbook in an earlier version of Excel, in this case Excel 2013

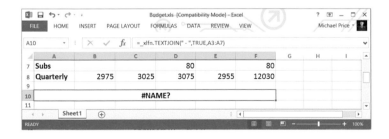

Select the cell with the formula containing the new function and you'll see _xlfn. added as a prefix to the function name, indicating the function is not known in this version of Excel.

When the formula is executed, the result is a #NAME? error, confirming that the function is not known.

In each case, the vertical references for the List range are specified with absolute addresses (for example, $B2:$B13), making it possible to copy the formula down for other values.

Compatibility Report

If the Compatibility Checker shows a number of issues:

1 Scroll the **Summary** list to review each issue

2 Alternatively, click **Copy to New Sheet**

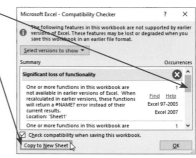

To invoke the Compatibility Checker without saving the file, select **File**, **Info**, **Check for Issues**, then select **Check Compatibility**.

From the Compatibility Checker you can choose the versions of Excel for which to display issues in the Compatibility Report.

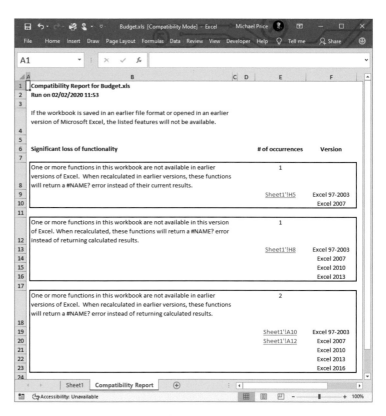

The Compatibility Report worksheet is added, showing all the issues identified for the active version of Excel.

For each issue there is an explanation; you are told which versions of Excel are affected, and you are given a link to the location with the unknown function, so you can review and resolve each of the issues in turn.

Cube Category

The Excel Cube functions enable data from OLAP cubes (see page 146) to be brought into Excel to perform calculations. These functions are supported with a connection to Microsoft SQL Server 2005 Analysis Services or a later data source. The functions include:

CUBEKPIMEMBER

This uses arguments Connection, Kpi_name, Kpi_property and the optional Caption. It returns a key performance indicator (KPI) property and displays the KPI name in the cell.

CUBEMEMBER

This uses arguments Connection, Member_expression and the optional Caption. It returns a member or tuple from the cube, to validate that the member or tuple exists in the cube.

CUBEMEMBERPROPERTY

This uses arguments Connection, Member_expression and Property. It returns the value of a member property from the cube, to validate that a member name exists within the cube and to return the specified property for this member.

CUBERANKEDMEMBER

This uses arguments Connection, Set_expression, Rank and the optional Caption. It returns the specified Rank member in a set – for example, to specify the top three entries in turn.

CUBESET

This uses arguments Connection, Set_expression, and the optional Caption, Sort_order and Sort_by. It defines a calculated set of members or tuples by sending a set expression to the cube on the server, which creates the set, and then returns that set to Microsoft Excel.

CUBESETCOUNT

This uses the argument Set and gives the number of items in a set.

CUBEVALUE

This uses the argument Connection and the optional arguments Member_expression1, Member_expression2 etc., to give an aggregated value from the cube.

The Excel PowerPivot function creates a data source that is compatible with OLAP cubes, so it can also be used with the Cube functions.

Online Analytical Processing (OLAP) is a technology that is used to organize large business databases and support business intelligence.

A KPI is a quantifiable measurement, such as monthly gross profit or quarterly employee turnover, that is used to monitor an organization's performance.

OLAP Cubes

OLAP (Online Analytical Processing) is a computing method to extract and query data in order to analyze it from different points of view. To facilitate this analysis, data is collected from multiple data sources and stored in data warehouses then cleansed and organized into data cubes.

Each OLAP cube contains data categorized by dimensions (such as customers, geographic sales region, time period and product) derived by dimensional tables in the data warehouses. Dimensions are then populated by associated entry values (such as customer names, countries, dates and product types) that are organized hierarchically.

As an example, the quantities of product stored at various locations at a range of times could create a simple three-dimensional cube.

Don't forget

The term Cube is a misnomer since the data blocks can have any number of dimensions, almost always more than three. Furthermore, the OLAP cube is not symmetrical. Some dimensions may have few entries while other dimensions may have many entries.

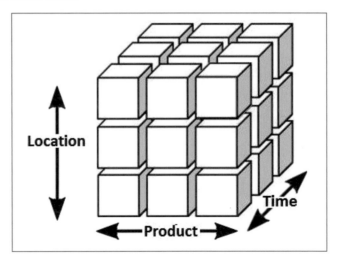

Typically, an OLAP cube will have more dimensions. An OLAP cube for sales data, for example, might include Sales Person, Sales Amount, Region, Customer Type, Month and Year.

OLAP cubes are often pre-summarized across dimensions to improve query time compared to the equivalent searches with relational databases.

Typical applications of OLAP include business reporting for sales, marketing, management reporting, business process management (BPM), budgeting, forecasting and financial reporting.

Web Category

The Web category was introduced in Excel 2013. It consists of three functions that allow your workbooks to access web services.

> ENCODEURL(Text)

Converts a string to a URL-enabled format, replacing disallowed characters with their UTF-8 equivalents.

> FILTERXML(Xml, Xpath)

Returns specific data from the XML content by using the specified XPath.

> WEBSERVICE(Url)

Returns data from a web service – a software service used to communicate between two devices on a network over HTTP using XML (Extensible Markup Language).

An example web service is the National Weather Service:

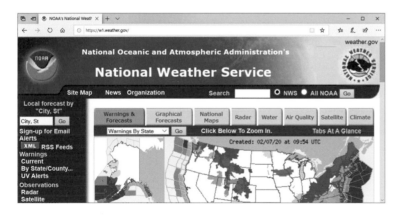

The detailed weather for a specific location such as New York City can be accessed via WEBSERVICE, using the URL for this web service with a code incorporating the location appended:

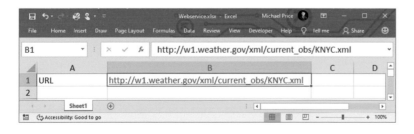

The characters that are encoded include:

	Space	%20
!	Exclamation Mark	%21
"	Quotation Mark	%22
#	Number Sign	%23
$	Dollar Sign	%24
/	Solidus	%2F
:	Colon	%3A

To see a local forecast, enter the city name (for example, New York) and select from the list of districts if more than one match is found.

...cont'd

Hot tip

This functionality was available in versions of Excel prior to Excel 2013 via the PowerUps Premium Suite add-in for Excel, which could be downloaded for free.

The encoded form of this URL is:

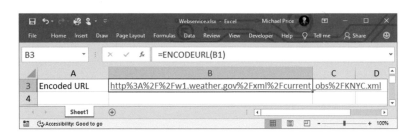

The WEBSERVICE function returns a long string of data related to the weather at the specified location:

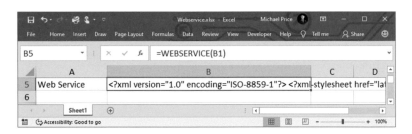

Don't forget

To identify component names visit the location web page and display its contents as XML using the keystroke **Ctrl** + **U**. Component names are enclosed in angled brackets – for example:

<title> .... </title> enclosing the associated data for the component.

You can retrieve individual components of the data for the specified location, using the FILTERXML function with the URL and the component name:

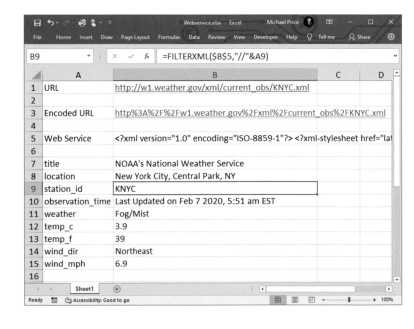

10 User Defined, Add-ins and Macros

If there are functions you need that are not installed in Excel by default, you can load Excel add-ins, some of which have associated User Defined Functions. There are also a number of COM add-ins. If these don't meet your needs, you can create your own custom functions in the form of macros, by recording a series of actions, or by using VBA (Visual Basic for Applications).

User Defined Category

When Excel is initially installed, there is no User Defined category specified:

The Euro Currency Tools and the Solver add-in both contain functions so will cause the User Defined category to be added or updated.

1 Select the **Formulas** tab, select **Insert Function** and click the **select a category** box

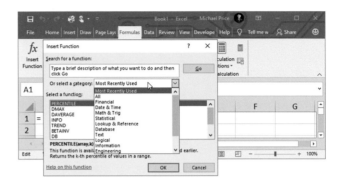

When you load Excel add-ins (see pages 55-56) and they contain functions, these will be shown in the User Defined category that will get added to the Insert Function dialog box.

2 Select **Insert Function** after you've loaded one of the add-ins that contain functions

3 If you load the Euro Currency Tools add-in, associated User Defined functions will be shown

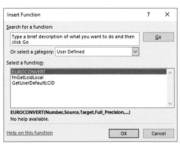

When you load the Solver add-in, you may see a large number of functions in a variety of languages added to the User Defined category.

4 If you load the Solver add-in (see page 154), a different group of User Defined functions will be shown

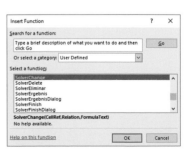

Analysis ToolPak Add-in

Select the **Developer** tab and load the **Analysis ToolPak add-in**, and you'll find that there will be no associated User Defined functions added.

However, the Analyze group is added to the **Data tab**, and the **Data Analysis** button is found in this group.

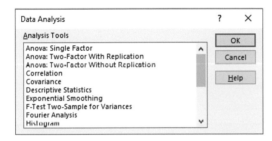

The functions that are included in the Analysis ToolPak are accessed from the Analyze group that gets added to the Data tab.

1 Select the **Data Analysis** button to explore the tools offered with this add-in

2 Scroll down to view the remaining tools

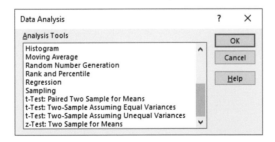

The Analysis ToolPak permits users to take advantage of complex statistical functions without necessarily understanding the equations that underlie those functions.

There are 19 different tools provided in the Analysis ToolPak. These include Descriptive Statistics (mean, mode, median, range, standard deviation etc.), Random Number Generation, Regression and statistical tools such as Anova (analysis of variance) and t-Test (tools for establishing the significance of the differences between groups of data).

Euro Currency Tools Add-in

The Euro Currency Tools allow you to format worksheet values as Euro currency, and to convert other currencies into Euros. You can find these tools in the Solutions group on the Formulas tab.

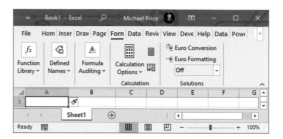

The Euro Currency add-in handles 17 currencies at this time that were previously in use in European countries that have now adopted the Euro. You'll find countries such as Belgium, France, Germany, Greece and Ireland in the list, but you won't find countries such as Denmark, Switzerland or the United Kingdom, which are in Europe but haven't adopted the Euro.

Don't forget

The Euro Currency Tools use the current conversion rates established by the EU. Microsoft will update the functions if the rates change, or if new countries are added to the list.

Hot tip

The Euro Currency Tools use the three-letter ISO codes for the various European currencies, as shown in the table.

Country	Currency	ISO code
Austria	schilling	ATS
Belgium	franc	BEF
Cyprus	pound	CYP
Estonia	kroon	EEK
EU state	euro	EUR
Finland	markka	FIM
France	franc	FRF
Germany	deutsche mark	DEM
Greece	drachma	GRD
Ireland	pound	IEP
Italy	lira	ITL
Luxembourg	franc	LUF
Malta	lira	MTL
Netherlands	guilder	NLG
Portugal	escudo	PTE
Slovakia	korura	SKK
Slovenia	tolar	SIT
Spain	peseta	ESP

You use the Euro Conversion tool to convert from one European currency to another, using the Euro as an intermediary. This is known as triangulation. For example, to convert French francs to Spanish pesetas, select the value for **Francs**, click **Euro Conversions**, and specify the conversion required.

Specify **Source range** and **Destination range**, select the currency to convert from and the currency to convert to, then click **OK**.

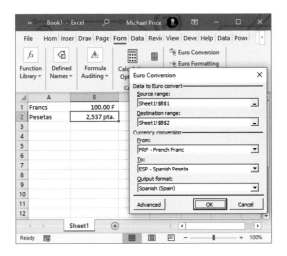

Select one or more cells that contain values and click **Euro Formatting** to apply Euro formatting to the selected cells.

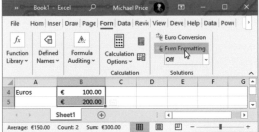

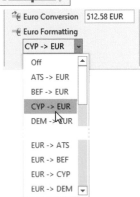

The drop-down box that you find below the two commands provides an instant conversion between any of the European currencies and their Euro equivalent, in either direction.

For example, to convert a value in Cyprus pounds to Euros, select the value and click **CYP->EUR**. The converted value appears alongside the Euro Conversion command.

153

Solver Add-in

When you load the Solver add-in, functions are added to the User Defined category, and the Solver button is placed in the Analyze group on the Data tab.

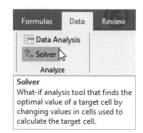

There is just one Solver tool. This is an optimization tool that can be used to determine how the desired outcome can be achieved by changing the assumptions in a model. It is a form of what-if analysis and is particularly useful when trying to determine the "best" outcome, given a set of more than two assumptions.

Don't forget

Solver applies the constraints you specify and changes the variable cells until the objective meets its specified value.

You use Solver to find a maximum or minimum or optimal value for a formula in the objective cell, subject to constraints, or limits, on the values of other cells on the worksheet. Solver adjusts the values in the variable cells to satisfy the constraints and produce the required value for the objective.

1 Select the **Data** tab and click **Solver** in the **Analyze** group

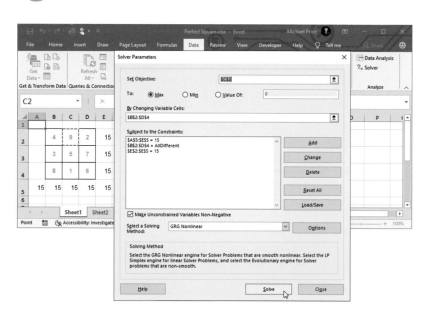

Hot tip

You can apply any of six constraint relationships (<=,=,>=,int,bin,dif) with a constraint value (or you can specify that the cells must be AllDifferent).

2 Specify the objective, the variables and the constraints and click **Solve** to find the solution

COM Add-ins

As described on pages 55-56, you can list the COM add-ins available using the Developer tab or by selecting **File**, **Options**, **Add-ins**. If you have Excel 365 installed, you will find three COM add-ins offered.

If you have Excel 2019 installed you'll find four COM add-ins. However, the Data Streamer add-in found in Excel 365 is not listed in Excel 2019.

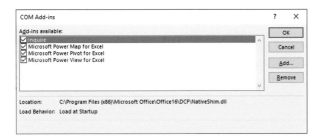

If you have upgraded to Office 2019, but would still like to use Data Streamer, search for "excel data streamer download" and follow the link to the Microsoft download site to add Data Streamer to your system.

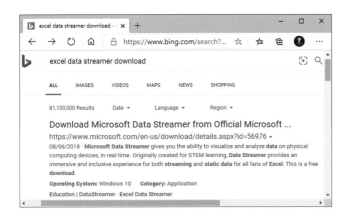

Select the Developer tab and click COM Add-ins in the Add-ins group.

At the Microsoft website, click the Download button and select the Setup.exe file that will be downloaded, to install the add-in.

Inquire Add-in

You install the Inquire add-in as one of the COM add-ins.

To use this function:

 1 Select the **Inquire** tab from the Ribbon

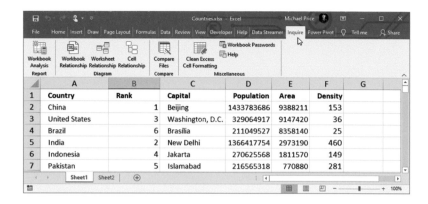

Using Inquire, you can analyze a workbook or compare two workbooks, cell by cell. The following commands are supported:

- Workbook Analysis
- Workbook Relationship
- Worksheet Relationship
- Cell Relationship
- Compare Files
- Clean Excess Cell Formatting
- Workbook Passwords

You can use the Workbook Analysis command to create an interactive report showing detailed information about the workbook structure, formulas, cells, ranges and warnings.

If you are using Workbook Analysis or Compare Files commands for workbooks that are password protected, you can avoid having to type the password each time those files are opened. You use the Password Manager to store the passwords for the workbooks you may want to access.

Power Pivot Add-in

With Power Pivot you can perform powerful data analysis and create sophisticated data models, collections of tables with relationships.

When you add Power Pivot, an associated tab is added to the Ribbon. To invoke Power Pivot:

1 Select **Power Pivot** from the Ribbon

Don't forget

Power Pivot allows you to handle very large data, not restricted by the limitations on the sizes of Excel worksheets.

2 Click **Manage** to open the Power Pivot window

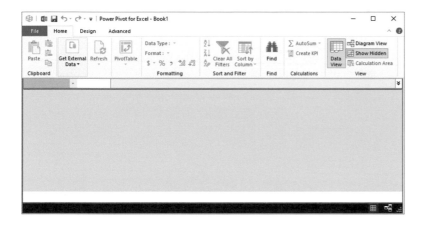

Hot tip

A companion feature to Power Pivot is Power Query, now known as Get & Transform Data. It is available by default and can be found on the Data tab.

3 Select **Get External Data** to import data from databases, data services and other sources

You can use the Table Import Wizard to filter the data, and use the data to create PivotTables and PivotCharts. You can then create relationships between tables, add calculations and build expressions, using the Data Analysis Expressions (DAX) expression language.

Power Map Add-in

Power Map, now known as 3D Maps, is a 3D data visualization tool that is used to map geographical data. It is located on the Insert tab, in the Tours group.

Open a workbook that has data that you want to map:

1 Click any cell in the data table

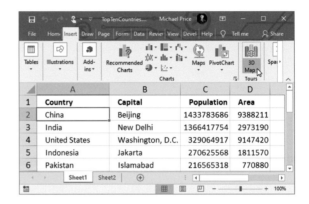

2 Click **Insert**, and then select the **3D Map** button

Don't forget

Clicking 3D Map for the first time automatically enables 3D Maps.

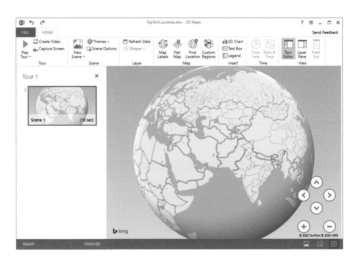

3D Maps uses Bing to geocode your data based on its geographic properties. This means that you will need to have an active internet connection while you are using 3D Maps.

Macros in Excel

If you have tasks that you often need to perform in your workbooks, and there are no add-ins to help, you can create your own functions in the form of Excel macros.

An Excel macro is a set of mouse clicks and keystrokes that you record, give a name to and save. When you run a saved macro, the recorded mouse clicks and keystrokes are executed in the same sequence as they were recorded.

To review the macro security settings:

1 Select **File**, **Options**, **Trust Center** and then click **Trust Center Settings...**

2 Select **Macro Settings** and note that by default all macros are disabled with notification

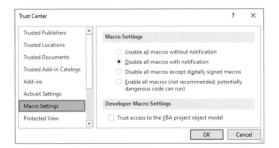

When you open a workbook that contains macros, you receive a warning and must enable content before opening that workbook.

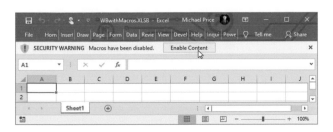

Macros help you to save time on repetitive tasks that are required to be performed frequently.

Because macros are so powerful, Excel includes security checks and controls to authenticate macros and to help prevent them being introduced into your system without your knowledge.

Macro Commands

To access the commands for viewing and recording macros:

1 Select the **View** tab, and click the arrow below the **Macros** button in the **Macros** group

By default, the Developer tab isn't displayed on the Tab bar, but you can easily add it using File, Options to customize the Ribbon.

2 Choose the **View Macros** or **Record Macro** option, and choose to **Use Relative References** in place of the default absolute references

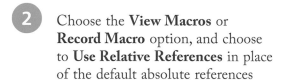

These options are also available from the **Developer** tab, along with the **Macro Security** and the **Visual Basic** options. To display the **Developer** tab:

1 Click the **File** tab and select **Options** (or press the keys **Alt + F + T**) and choose **Customize Ribbon**

160

You can view, run, edit and record macros from either the View tab or the Developer tab, but to create new macros or to change security settings, you must have the Developer tab displayed.

2 Click the **Developer** box in the **Main Tabs** section, and the **Developer** tab will be added to the Tab bar

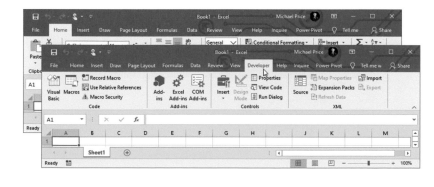

Recording Macros

Assume you want a macro to add author details to any workbook.

1 Open a blank workbook, and click cell A1

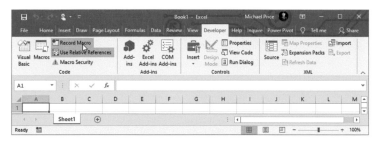

2 Select **Developer**, then **Use Relative References** and then **Record Macro** to start defining your macro

3 Enter a **Macro name**, specify a **Shortcut key** – e.g. **Shift + A** (with the **Ctrl** key added automatically)

4 Select **Personal Macro Workbook** to store the macro, and provide a **Description** for the macro, and then click **OK** to start recording

5 Carry out the required actions – e.g. type author details and press **Enter**, then click **Stop Recording**

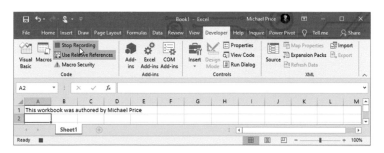

6 Close the workbook (no need to save it) but be sure to **Save** the **Personal Macro Workbook** when you close your Excel session

You can also select View, Record Macro, or click the **Record Macro** button found on the left of the status bar.

The first character of the macro name must be a letter, followed by letters, numbers or underscores. Spaces are not allowed.

Excel shortcuts already use most **Ctrl + lowercase letter**, so it is better to use capital letters for new macro shortcuts.

The macro is saved using VBA (Visual Basic for Applications) – see pages 162-163.

161

Using VBA

You can create macros using the VBA (Visual Basic for Applications) language. For example:

1 Ensure that the **Developer** tab is displayed (see page 160)

2 Select the **Developer** tab and then select **Visual Basic**

(see page 160)

You can search on the internet for examples of VBA coding. For example, **excel. offthegrid.com** gives the coding for 100 Excel VBA Macros, or check out Visual Basic in easy steps.

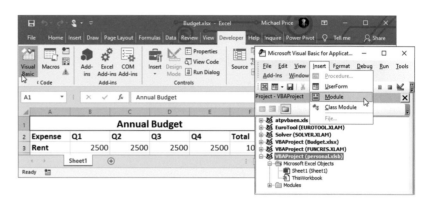

3 Select **VBAProject (personal.xlsb)** and then choose **Insert, Module**

4 In the code window for the module, type or copy/paste the code for your macro

This macro sets the CenterHeader as the current date for prints of a workbook in which the macro is run. It can easily be modified to specify other headers or footers on the printed page.

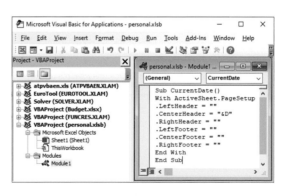

```
Sub CurrentDate()
With ActiveSheet.PageSetup
.LeftHeader = ""
.CenterHeader = "&D"
.RightHeader = ""
.LeftFooter = ""
.CenterFooter = ""
.RightFooter = ""
End With
End Sub
```

5 When you have entered and checked the VBA code for your macro, select **File** and then click **Close and Return to Microsoft Excel**

...cont'd

To see the new macro in action:

1 Open one of your workbooks and select **Developer, Macros**

2 Select the **CurrentDate** macro and click **Run**

3 The center header for prints will now be adjusted to show the current date

Hot tip

The **CurrentDate** will have been saved in the **Personal** folder ready to use when required.

To see the effect of the macro:

1 Choose a selection of the current worksheet

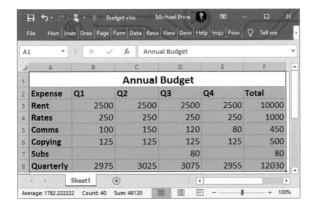

163

2 Select **File, Print** and choose **Print Selection** in Settings

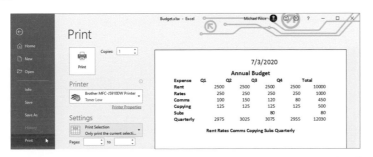

Don't forget

Save the workbook to retain the modified center header or just print the pages required and close without saving to leave the header unchanged.

You'll see that the current date is shown as the center header for the selection printout.

Macros on the Toolbar

You can invoke a macro using its shortcut key. You can also run a macro by selecting the **Macros** button from the **View** tab or the **Developer** tab. To make macros immediately accessible, you can add the **View Macros** option to the Quick Access Toolbar:

1 Select **File**, **Options**, then click **Quick Access Toolbar** and choose **View Macros** from **Popular Commands**

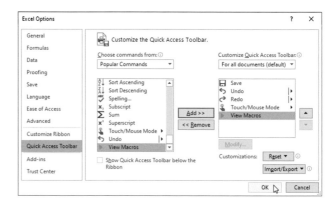

Don't forget

Alternatively, you could right-click one of the **Macros** buttons and select **Add to Quick Access Toolbar**.

164

2 Click **Add**, and then click **OK**

The **View Macros** icon will now be displayed on the **Quick Access Toolbar**, always visible and ready to use.

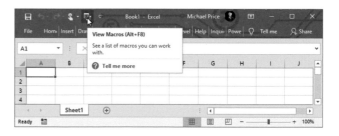

Beware

If you want to add or change a shortcut key for a macro, select the macro using the **Macros** button and then click the **Options...** button.

Run
Step Into
Edit
Create
Delete
Options...
Cancel

3 Whenever you want to use a macro, click the **View Macros** button on the toolbar, select the macro you need, and click **Run**

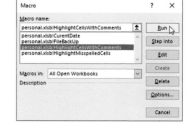

Of course, you can still use any of the other ways of running macros.

...cont'd

You can also add macros as individual icons on the **Quick Access Toolbar**. To do this:

1 Open the **Excel Options**, select **Quick Access Toolbar** and then **Choose commands from Macros**

Macros can also be associated with graphics or with hot spots on the worksheet to make them easily accessible.

2 Scroll down to the macros you want to add, select the first one and click **Add**

3 Each macro you add is assigned the same icon. You can click **Modify** to choose a different icon

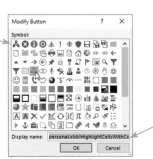

You can choose to change the **Display name** for any macro that you add.

4 The icon for each macro added will be placed on the **Quick Access Toolbar**

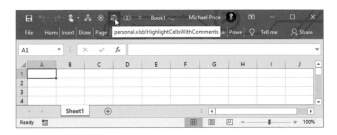

5 Hover the mouse pointer over an icon on the **Quick Access Toolbar**, and the **Screen Tip** shows the name of the macro, which runs whenever you click that icon

Macros Step by Step

If you want to know exactly what actions a particular macro is taking, you can choose to run it one step at a time.

1 Select **Macros** from **View** or **Developer**, choose the macro you want to review, and click **Step Into**

 *does not apply*

Open a workbook within which the macro is available, before selecting the **Step Into** option.

2 Press **F8** repeatedly to run through the macro code, one line at a time

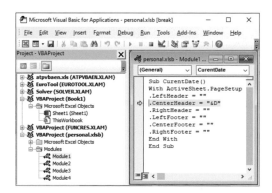

3 Select **Debug** to see all the testing options available, including a specification of breakpoints

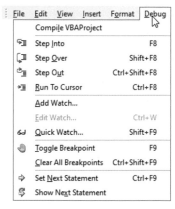

A **Breakpoint** is a macro statement at which execution will automatically stop. The breakpoints you set will not be saved with the code when you exit.

4 Press **F5** to continue to the next breakpoint or to complete the macro, if no breakpoints have been set

5 To finish and leave **Debug**, select **File, Close and Return to Microsoft Excel**

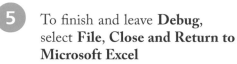

11

Support and References

Excel provides functions to back up and save your workbooks. You can use ready-made templates to give you a head start creating workbooks. There are more Excel resources at Microsoft Office Support and other websites. You can share your workbooks via print or as PDFs.

Backup

It can be useful to make copies of your workbooks, especially if you will be making significant changes. To do this within Excel:

1 Select **File** and click **Open** (or press **Ctrl + O**)

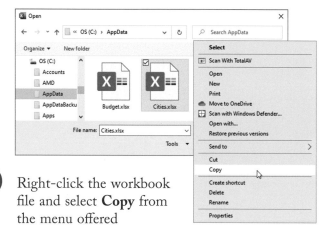

Hot tip

The same menus appear if you right-click the workbook file from within File Explorer.

2 Right-click the workbook file and select **Copy** from the menu offered

3 Switch to the backup folder, right-click an empty area and select **Paste** from the menu displayed

Don't forget

If there is no existing version in the backup folder, the selected file is simply copied there, with no messages displayed.

4 You are warned if the backup folder already contains a version of that file

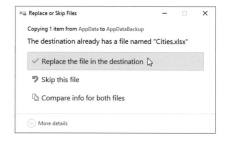

5 Compare file info to identify which version you want

168

AutoRecover

Excel automatically saves your workbooks on a regular basis. To review the settings:

1 Select **File**, **Options** and then click **Save**

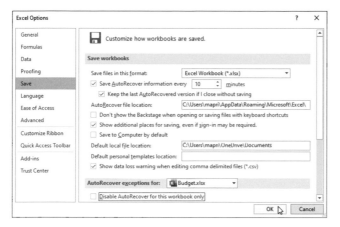

Excel will automatically save your workbook periodically, by default every 10 minutes, and can recover changes if your system shuts down in the middle of updating.

2 Check the values, including the frequency for **AutoRecover**, then click **OK** to save any changes

If your system should shut down without you having saved your recent changes, the next time you start Windows and Excel you are given the opportunity to retrieve your changes, up to the last **AutoRecover**.

The **Document Recovery** task pane can display up to three versions of your file, with the most recent at the top.

3 Select a recovered entry, click the arrow and choose **Open**, **Save As...** or **Delete** as appropriate

4 Alternatively, you can select the original version to discard changes

Excel will keep the last AutoRecover entry, even if you deliberately close Excel without saving, so you can still retrieve your latest changes.

Templates

Hot tip

You can save effort, and discover new aspects of Excel, if you base your new workbooks on the templates that are provided in Excel.

1 Click the **File** tab, and then click **New** to be offered the blank workbook and suggestions for templates

2 Review the example templates, or select a category such as "Financial Management" to see more templates

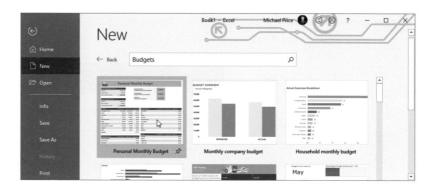

Don't forget

The template will be downloaded and a workbook will be opened ready for use, or you can make any changes you wish, if it doesn't exactly meet your requirements.

3 Select the template you want to use – "Personal Monthly Budget", for example – review the description provided, and then click **Create**

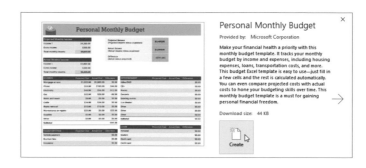

4 The **Start** worksheet provides a brief introduction

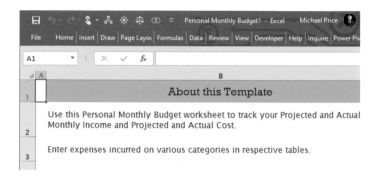

5 The **Personal Monthly Budget** worksheet contains sample data to illustrate the operations of the template

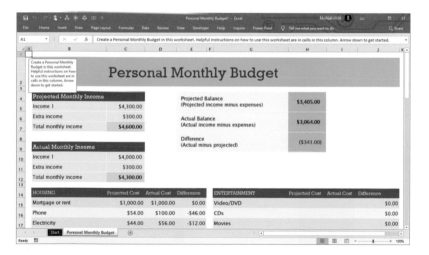

Hot tip

Review the data, and then experiment with changes to the values, to see the effect.

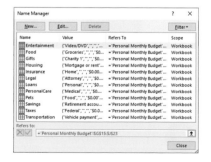

6 Select **Formulas** and click **Name Manager** (or press **Ctrl + F3**), to see the names defined in the workbook, and their values

Don't forget

To keep the results, you'll need to save the workbook – the default name is the template name, with a number appended.

Online Templates

You can search online templates to find those that relate to the particular topic you have in mind.

1 Select **File**, **New**, and click **Search for online templates**, enter a search term (e.g. "fitness") and click the magnifier

The last template that you downloaded and used will be listed in the featured templates ready for possible re-use.

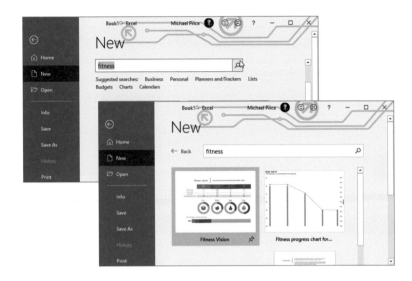

2 Matching templates will be listed, with their titles and illustrative images

3 Scroll down to review all the results offered

The templates may be in compatibility mode, if they were originally designed for a previous version of Excel.

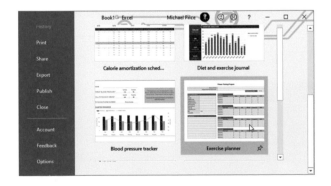

4 Identify a template that you'd like to investigate, and select it to create a workbook on your system. See page 170 for an example

...cont'd

You can amend the selected template and save the revised copy in your Documents library for later use.

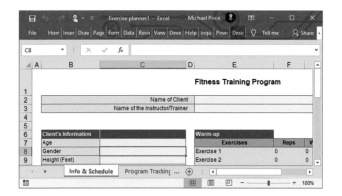

 Hot tip

If the template contains macros or VBA code, you will need to save it as an **Excel Macro-Enabled Template (*.xltm)**.

1. Select **File, Save As**, select your **Documents** folder and choose the type of **Excel Template (*.xltx)**

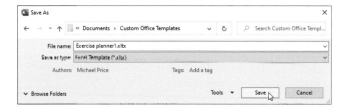

2. It will be saved in **Documents/Custom Office Templates**

3. Select **File, New, Personal** to view your templates

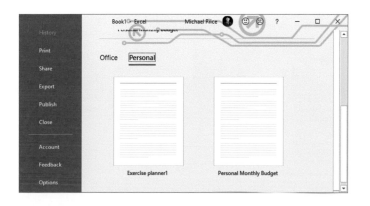

 Don't forget

You can also save an Excel workbook as a template to use as the basis for other workbooks. Such templates are also saved in the **Personal** area.

Internet Resources

The internet is a prolific source of advice and guidance for Excel users at all levels. Here are some websites that may prove useful:

1 Go to **support.office.com** and select the **Excel** icon

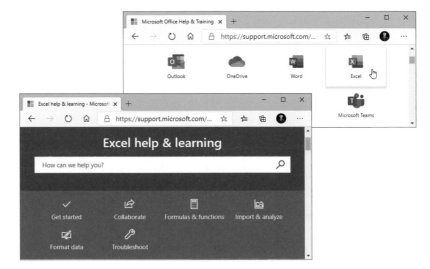

A search on google.com with Excel-related search terms will result in millions of matches, so it will be easier to start from a more focused website such as **Microsoft Office Support**.

2 Review advice for getting started and using Excel formulas and functions

3 Scroll on down for a variety of links to help you to explore Excel and get to know its features

The actual links and content for the Office Support web pages change over time, but you should expect to find links similar to those shown here.

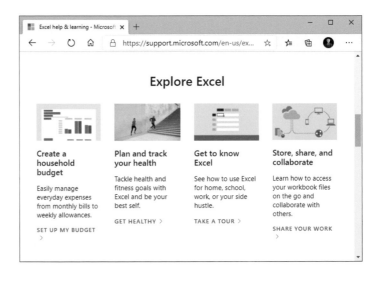

4 You'll also find up-to-date information related to Excel in the **Trending Topics** section

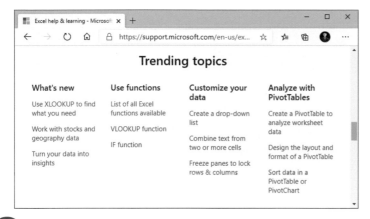

The **Trending Topics** highlight some particular features and functions that you may find useful, and also provides a link to the list of all Excel functions available.

5 Scroll on down to find links that will help you to submit questions and get answers

6 Click **Contact Us** to send your question to the Microsoft Office Support group

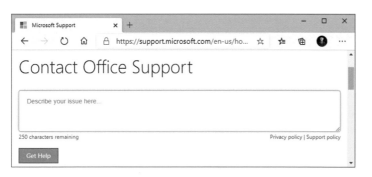

You can send questions directly to the **Office Support Group**, though you can't go into much detail since the question length is limited.

7 Describe your issue (in no more than 250 characters) and select **Get Help**

Office Community

You can explore the answers that other users have provided for your area of interest:

1 At the **support.office.com** website select the **Ask the Community** link (see page 175)

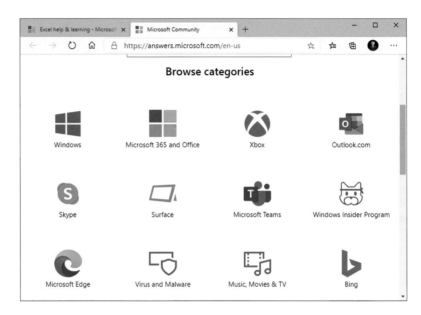

(see page 175)

You can post questions, follow discussions and share your knowledge, on a total of 22 different categories.

2 Select the category **Microsoft 365 and Office**

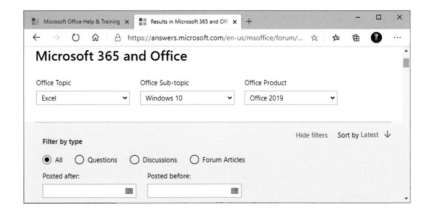

You can view all entries or filter by Questions, Discussions and Forum Articles. You can also specify posting dates, Before and After.

3 Set **Excel** as the Office Topic, **Windows 10** as the Office Sub-topic and **Office 2019** as the Office Product

Microsoft MVPs (most valued professionals) can also be useful sources of help and information.

1 To find out about the MVPs that are in your area, go to **mvp.microsoft.com**

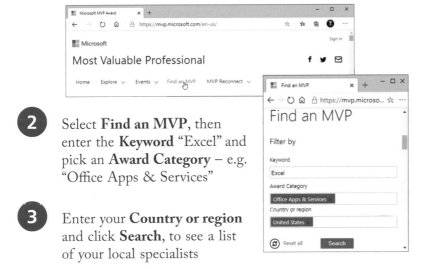

There is a link for each MVP listed that gives biographical details and accounts of recent activities that relate to the area of interest that you selected.

2 Select **Find an MVP**, then enter the **Keyword** "Excel" and pick an **Award Category** – e.g. "Office Apps & Services"

3 Enter your **Country or region** and click **Search**, to see a list of your local specialists

If you are interested in creating Excel functions and macros, you should visit the Office and Excel developers' centers:

4 Go to **devcloper.microsoft.com/office** and select **Excel**

You'll find that many items reference Excel 2016, 2013 or previous versions. These items will often be just as applicable when you are running Excel 2019.

Wikipedia

For an overview of Excel history and features, you should read the Wikipedia entry for Excel:

1 Go to **www.wikipedia.com**

2 Search for "microsoft excel"

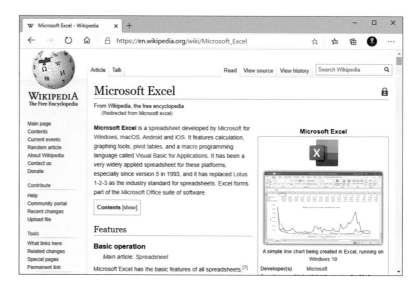

This article covers the versions of Excel for the supported operating environments, which include Windows, Macintosh, OS/2, Mobile and Excel for the web.

A full list of citations is provided, along with general sources and external links. There are also references to other related Wikipedia articles.

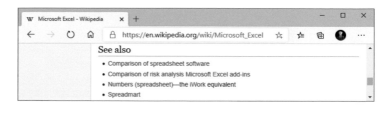

Excel Help

For assistance in using Excel you can take advantage of the **Help** function. To access **Help**:

1 Press the **F1** key to open the **Help** panel

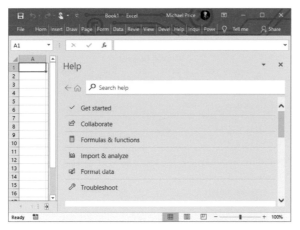

2 Scroll down to view the **Featured help** selection

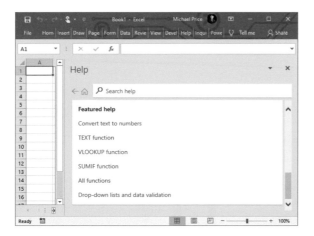

3 Alternatively, click **Tell Me** on the Tab bar (or press the **Alt + Q** keys), and type the topic you need help with – for example, "float"

You'll get a list of related Help entries, plus a Smart Lookup that finds associated results from various online sources.

You can also access Excel Help by selecting **Help** on the Tab bar then clicking the **Help** icon.

Select any entry on the Help panel to expand that topic and to find links to related subtopics.

Save Workbook Online

You can store workbooks and other documents online, and access them via the Office Online apps, or share them with other users. To save a workbook to OneDrive from within Excel:

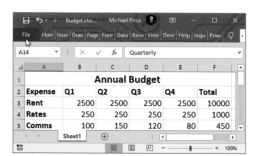

1 Open the workbook, click **File**, and select **Save As**

2 Select the OneDrive folder for the current user and double-click to explore the OneDrive contents

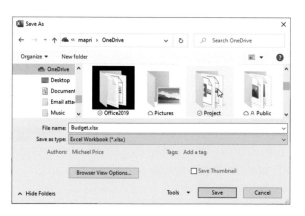

3 Select the OneDrive folder where you'll put the workbook – "Project", for example – and double-click to open the folder

4 Amend the workbook name if required, and click **Save**

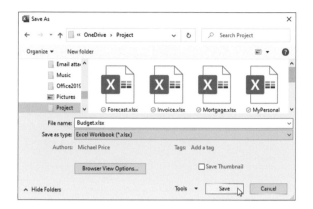

Hot tip

Once you have saved the workbook to your OneDrive, close it from within Excel and you can open it from within your browser (see pages 182-183).

With the workbook on your OneDrive, you can now access it via your browser, even on computers that do not have a copy of the Excel 2019 application installed.

1 Go online to **office.com** and sign in using the email address that is associated with your Microsoft Account

2 Scroll down and double-click the **OneDrive** icon

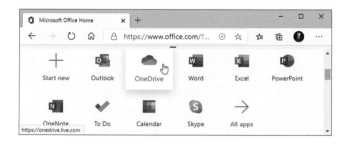

Don't forget

At the Office Online website you can work with documents from Word, Excel, PowerPoint and OneNote, whether or not you have Office 2019 on your computer.

3 The **OneDrive** folders and files are displayed

Excel Online

You can have up to 5GB of free storage on your OneDrive. You can purchase additional storage for an annual fee (correct at the time of printing).

You can right-click a file or folder in your OneDrive and select **Share**, to send a link by email to allow other users to access the workbook via their browsers or via Excel 2019 if installed.

1 From your OneDrive, double-click the folder that contains the workbook you want to view

2 When the folder opens, right-click the required workbook to display the options that are available

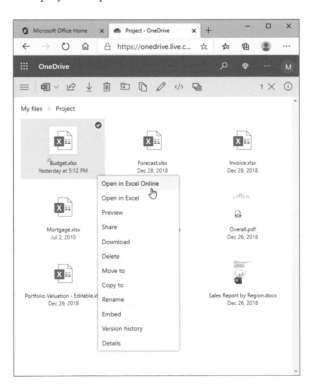

3 Select **Open in Excel Online** to open the workbook in your browser

4 The workbook opens in your browser ready to edit

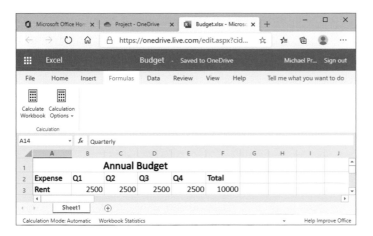

Note that not all features of Excel 2019 are supported in the Excel Online app. However, you can switch to the full version:

5 Click the **Open in Desktop App** tab to edit the workbook in Excel 2019

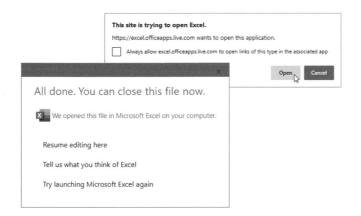

6 Click **Open**, and then you can close the browser copy of the workbook, and edit it with the desktop app

When you try to open a workbook in Excel Online, you'll be warned if it is already open. You aren't allowed to edit it in Excel Online, but you can use **reading view**.

You need a supported version of Microsoft Excel on your computer to open the workbook in the desktop app.

To share data with others who don't have access to Excel or the Office Online apps, you can present the information in a Microsoft Office Word document (as illustrated here), or in a PowerPoint presentation.

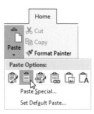

You can paste the data as a table, retaining the original formatting, or using styles from the Word document, as shown. Alternatively, paste the data as a picture or tab-separated text. There are also options to maintain a link with the original worksheet.

Excel in Word

To add data from your Excel worksheet to your Word document:

1 In Excel, select the worksheet data, and press **Ctrl** + **C** (or select **Home** and click **Copy**, from the **Clipboard** group)

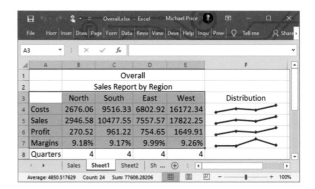

2 Click in the Word document, and press **Ctrl** + **V** (or select **Home** and click **Paste**, from the **Clipboard** group)

3 From **Paste Options**, select the type of paste you want

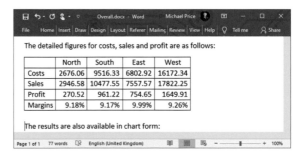

4 The data from the workbook is inserted in the document

...cont'd

To copy an Excel chart to your Word document:

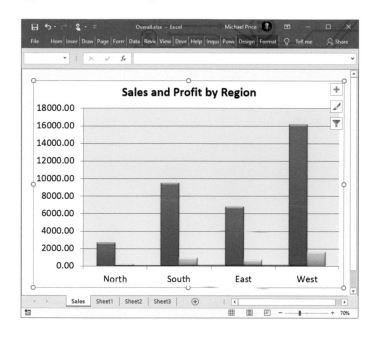

Apply any text styles or chart formatting required, before you copy the chart to the clipboard.

1 In Excel, select the chart on the worksheet or chart sheet, and press **Ctrl + C** (or select **Home**, **Copy**)

2 In the Word document, click where you want the chart, and press **Ctrl + V** (or select **Home**, **Paste**)

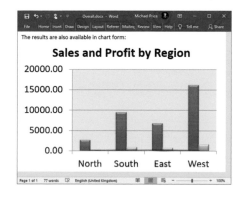

You can choose to simply paste the chart as a **Picture**. Alternatively, you may choose a paste option – **Keep Source Formatting**, or **Use Destination Theme**, or **Embed Workbook** or **Link Data**.

Publish as PDF or XPS

To send data to others who do not have Excel or Word, you can publish the workbook in Adobe Acrobat PDF format, or in XPS format. The recipient just needs to have a suitable viewing app, such as Acrobat Reader, Microsoft Reader, or XPS Viewer.

1 Open the workbook in Excel, click the **File** tab, and then click **Save As** to choose the file type

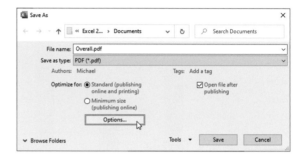

186

2 Select the **Save as type** box and choose PDF or XPS

3 Click the **Options** button, to set the scope – e.g. **Active sheet(s)** or **Entire workbook** – and click **OK**

4 Check **Open file after publishing**, then click **Save** to create and display the PDF or XPS file

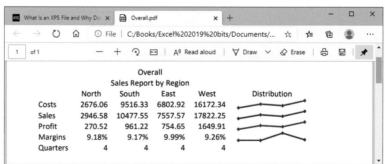

When you save your workbooks as PDF or XPS files, you can be sure that the files you share will retain exactly the data and format that you intended for them.

Index

D